SEEING THROUGH WALLS

A journal of post-meditation reflection

SEEING THROUGH WALLS

A journal of post-meditation reflection

Joseph C. Sturgeon II

ACKNOWLEDGEMENTS

I would like to take a few sentences here and give credit and honor where it is due. I would like to personally thank Dr. Adonijah Ogbonnaya. His help and mastery in the meditative arena (among others) is unmatched and something we admire greatly. He has helped shape my marriage as mystics. Without exaggeration this work would not have been possible without him and his help as we would not have understood the depths we were plumbing without his insight, resources and knowledge. Much of the structure we begin to address here began with Dr O. He is a spiritual mentor, friend and one of the most gracious people we have ever had the privilege of meeting. He also demonstrably loves Jesus Christ in his personal and daily life more than anyone I have met. Thank you Dr. O.

I would also like to thank my wife who without this would not be possible. Those of you who know her will see where she interjected. Those would be the good parts! She was the idea and execution of this work and is deserving of thanks.

Lastly I would like to thank my good friend Chris Blackeby. Some of the stories you will read in this book were with him on adventures. Chris, you are one of the most intentional, loving, un-compromised people I have known and have helped more people that I love dearly than anyone else I have met. (Also, my passport still has room so I think you are winning our competition). Thanks bro.

Joseph

"Christ with me, Christ before me,
 Christ behind me,
 Christ in me,
 Christ beneath me,
 Christ above me,
 Christ on my right, Christ on my left,
 Christ when I lie down,
 Christ when I sit down, Christ when I arise,
 Christ in the heart of every man who thinks of me,
 Christ in the mouth of everyone who speaks of me,
 Christ in every eye that sees me,
 Christ in every ear that hears me."

St. Patrick

TABLE OF CONTENTS

INTENTION SETTING

My intention with this journal is

WELCOME

Welcome to *Seeing through Walls*, your post-meditation journal.

There are few words to describe the impact journals have had on the world. From the journal of Marco Polo inspiring Christopher Columbus on his journey, to the sketches of Leonardo da Vinci, to a detailed look into struggles of Ludwig van Beethoven in dealing with depression and deafness - all while producing music that changed the world. Churchill's "finest hour" was scribed in a journal. General George S. Patton's most famous quotes like "You can be what you will to be," and "Always do more than what is required of you," were all written in a journal. These journals are the outward projection of the inward thoughts of the most famous and inspiring people ever to live. They are a sneak peek into the minds of the world's most brilliant composers, warriors, poets and even the "common folk." A journal is a place where dreams are unlocked, visions are inspired and tears are shed. Journals are painfully honest and breathtakingly brilliant; they are a level playing field where normal people like you and I discover the veiled brilliance of the secrets hidden within, only to find out we are not normal and the playing field is stacked in our favor.

Journaling itself is a journey into one's self to discover hidden truth and mysteries. The Bible talks about how "It is the glory of the lord to conceal a matter but the glory of Kings to search it out." Where did God conceal those mysteries if not inside us? For Claire and I, journals are an irreplaceable tool that has helped in our journey - some of which we will print and give to our grandchildren as part of their inheritance. Our Patreon channel, *"The Ancient Quest"* was birthed from ideas we had while journaling. It is not ok for the breakthroughs we have attained and the knowledge we have gained to be lost. It may be 200 years before someone truly understands it but one day, one of our descendants will pick it up and the time will come for them to carry on the work and they will start leap years ahead of those around them. Why? Because we took the time to write it down and the necessary steps to preserve it.

We would like to invite you into this process with us. Contained within this book are the very simple, very practical steps we took at the beginning to develop within ourselves the discipline of journaling. Some days there is much to say, some days there is very little but we have included enough structure to help you produce something daily. It is our joy to welcome you to the journey. We have prayed over and engaged every word written in here in the desire that it will produce in you what has benefited us for so many years.

So let the adventure begin,

> Joseph and Claire

WHY IS JOURNALING IMPORTANT AND HOW TO CONSISTENTLY PRACTICE JOURNALING

The most common questions we are asked are "how do I see in the spirit?", "how do I see more?" or "why, when I meditate alone, do I see nothing?" The presence of God is an incredible thing, when it interacts with Wisdom it produces sparks of light that become 'flashes'. Eventually, if we pay attention, we can hold those lightning flashes in stillness until they open themselves to us and that which is contained within. The understanding of the above becomes infused into our being. We may not always be aware that there is a flash, yet when we experience a moment of infused insight that could only come from God (a revelation of something far beyond our experience, our knowledge or our own understanding) it is in those moments that we have in fact grasped the flash within our being and held it, even for a split second, in mid motion before it passes. Meditation teaches us an increase in the awareness of these sparks and flashes and trains our focus and will to grasp these flashes.

Physically writing and journaling is valuable and beneficial in many ways. We have listed a few that we think might interest you.

1. Enhances the Remembrance.

   James, in the Bible, describes disobeying the word like looking into the mirror and then forgetting the image. Often our encounters, experiences, peace, growth and even the mental edifices we build become forgotten as we move through our day to the next thing. Writing about the insight forces you to slow your mind down and focus on the specific aspects you encounter. It brings them from the subconscious aspects of your mind to the conscious forefront. It causes a solidifying of what you have seen, felt, experienced. By writing, your mind revisits what you have experienced or seen. This is the beginning of learning to "see in the spirit." Clear encounters are the result of a trained mind that sees detail through practice and discipline.

2. Causes Growth

   After your meditation, journaling using prompts and questions can cause you to focus on things you might not have noticed before. Jesus, in the Gospels, often used questions to draw out that which was hidden beneath the surface. The Jewish way of learning often involves questions that force the mind to consider multiple perspectives. Growth is the product of an open mind that adapts quickly to change.

3. Trains Your Brain

Physically writing also gives weight and value to that which you might dismiss. For example, perhaps when meditating on the heart you experience or sense some kind of angelic movement. You don't necessarily know their name, function or purpose. Perhaps you can't see them but you just sense that something is there. This is a starting point to access more! The first time you saw an apple and your parents said "apple," you probably couldn't repeat it immediately. In fact, it probably took a few more times of seeing the apple and having the word "apple," said for you to grasp that the red fruit is an apple. It is the same with seeing in the spirit. When you chose to acknowledge that you felt or sensed something when you did 'x' or 'y', even if you don't know what it is, it says this is valuable enough to focus my attention on and becomes an invite for noticing that sense again. Consistency in noticing and paying attention to that sense will over time show you what that is and what is going on. Your brain recognizing spiritual information as relevant is a product of training and consistency.

4. Additional Access and an Ability to Dive Deeper.

We are part of an instant culture. We want to understand everything and know everything in a split-second while only holding the flash for just a moment. Although everything can be infused in mere moments, it is not often that our mental eyes can pick up all the details. It is the same as if we are to open a text book and glance over a page. Perhaps we pick up some diagrams and some text but it takes a few reads to understand that page, to understand how that page fits into the textbook and what aspects of that content is not present on that page that also needs to be considered. Journaling is a way of revisiting something in order to dive deeper into it.

5. Body Memory.

The ancients used to write with scented ink because physically writing something creates a body memory that becomes ingrained into you. Adding a scent to it causes your mind to shift to that subject when you smell that specific scent. It causes additional alertness. By physically writing something down, say for instance an 'I am' statement, solidifies that statement in your physical body. Now when you are placed in a situation and you need to remember who you are, it becomes much more present than merely a passing thought during meditation. Body memory concretizes that which was previously elusive.

HOW TO USE THIS JOURNAL

"Fill your paper with the breathings of your heart." William Wordsworth

This is your journal, these are your thoughts, your reflections, your visions and there is no right or wrong in this space - only the ever-present love of God flowing towards you. Our intention in creating this journal is to help you reflect and ask yourself thoughtful questions that increase and add value to the beauty discovered in your meditations. We have created a structure for this journal but in no way, shape or form is this structure intended to be restrictive. The structure provided can be held loosely or adhered to strictly. No matter your preference this is your personal journey, so rather than forcing something, allow the freedom of His breath to guide you through these pages.

Structure:

This journal is split into 3 components and each component lasts for 28 days (yes, not a full month, as it gives you a few days in case you skip or forget to journal that day). Each component or section has a theme but it is not crucial for you to do them in order. Remember, this is your journal, so use your intuition and decide which of the three aspects is important for you for now and pick that one. Same applies to the prompts. If you don't feel like the one for that day is particularly useful then pick another one from the many suggestions at the end of each section.

Part 1: The Soul

The first 28 days is about self and soul. It incorporates the identity, mind, heart, generational blessings and your purpose. The intent is that through reflection, prompts and a series of meditations you will find out more about yourself and your beautiful unique soul's make up. You will begin to discover how your unique soul is meant to contribute to this world and leave a lasting impact on the Earth. Learning to create identity statements from a place of deep intimacy and rest are a focal point of this month and are continued through into the next two months.

Part 2: Becoming a Creator

The second part of this journal s about becoming a creator. Focusing on the four-letter name of God and the name of Jesus, to understand at a deeper level God's interconnection with all of creation. In addition to this part two also looks at the role of angels within the process of creating and the elemental substance that man is given to mold, shape and structure creation by connecting it to the name of God.

Part 3: Creating Equilibriums

The third part revolves around harmonizing seemingly opposing concepts both within ourselves and globally, such as mercy and judgment, life and death and resurrection, light and darkness, provision and drought. Consider impressionist paintings; their purpose was to capture the light, but in order to portray the light they needed to harmonize the shadows within the painting to create something of true beauty. When we can harmonize these components, we cause beauty to emerge.

Weekly Agenda

a.) Inspiration

Getting a bit more specific, each week begins with a description of the meditation focus for that week. The purpose is to inspire and expand your mind and heart with these descriptions and to give your glimpses into the poetic beauty that is contained within creation and the way that God has created.

b.) Identity Statement

Each week begins with creating an 'I am' statement. An entire section in Part One is dedicated to the importance of creating 'I am' statements and how to create, write and structure them according to the pattern that Jesus sets in the gospels. These statements and declarations are pivotal in the growth of identity and establishing your will - in knowing who you are at the very core of your being. The spirit realm responds to who you are and not what you do. By writing and speaking declarations of who you are, you establish at both a conscious and unconscious level your true identity, solidifying it as a magnetic beacon to which the world responds. Writing these 'I am' statements down shows you how your identity evolves over time and helps you look back and see how God establishes that aspect of your identity. From there you move to the next aspect.

c.) Meditation Planning

In addition to these weekly inspirations, a chart is provided to help plan the meditations you desire to do in the week ahead. The weekly chart is provided for two reasons. The first is to define the focus of meditation that day. Although each week has a general theme, sometimes there are specific aspects of that theme that you may want to focus on, or a specific 'I am' statement. Stating the focus helps set your intention prior to meditation. The second purpose is to help define the specific aspects or technique of meditation that you wish to grow in that week. Some examples of this include breathing and focusing on being in the present, incorporating relaxation techniques to enhance meditation, creating the cube, reciting a specific bible verse, chanting the letters of the name of God and saying the names of God. It could be just a matter of increasing the time spent meditating each day rather than a different type of meditation. There are endless possibilities (for more ideas see *'The Ancient Quest'* on Patreon). The value of the weekly planning method is to help you keep track of your meditation practice, to ensure that the type of meditation is adding value and that you are growing daily.

Again, it is important to restate that while having an initial meditation plan is valuable, everyone is different. Some thrive with structure, to some structure feels like a lack of freedom. The important thing is that your meditation draws from your relationship with God and that you feel free to embrace His movement and grow, spend time and develop yourself in the area that God is growing you. The prompts and planning are merely keys and help to define the focus but nothing trumps the love of God and His unique path for and with you.

Identity Statement

I am... the repairer of worlds

which accomplishes (associated action)
I draw from the inner depths of divinity and bring it into the physical realm through love and joy lifting those around me into the future.

DAY	FOCUS POINT	MEDITATION PLAN
SUNDAY	Harmonization through beauty	4 breaths in; 6 out
MONDAY	Spirit as the wind that modulates the waters	Engage John 3:8
TUESDAY	Holy Spirit as something that increases the fire	Meditate on the Name Ruach Hakodesh
WEDNESDAY	Breath to calm waters of the soul	In mind's eye, breath calmness over the waters
THURSDAY	Breath as a mechanism of transport through the worlds	4 breaths in; 6 out in cycles of four
FRIDAY	The ability of God's name to calm the waters	Meditate on each of the letters of a Name of God
SATURDAY	John 14:27; Create an I am statement about peace	Meditate on John 14:27

Notes

DAILY JOURNAL ENTRIES

And finally, there is the daily journal. The core practice of the daily journaling seeks to answer 6 main questions:

1. The Daily Question/Prompt

Each day begins with a prompt or question to consider a specific aspect of the weekly topic. These questions were created with the intention of prompting or encouraging you to look again, look deeper and observe something that perhaps you did not notice. We have also created additional questions at the end of each section. Should the questions we have included not elicit your desired exploration then possibly there is a different one that would serve you better. These are not prescriptive but rather ideas to help inspire understanding. This question can be thought about throughout the day, answered in your mind, in the section of what I am noticing, in the general writing area (spiritual insight) or completely discarded. It is important to do what feels right for you.

2. What am I celebrating?

Gratitude is like the perpetual dawn. Celebration can be likened to causing the Sun to rise throughout the day and exuberant joy is critical in manifestation. By turning towards gratitude and celebrating at the start of our day, we set joy and satisfaction at the beginning of our day. We expand our joy and our sunrise throughout the day, causing a bursting forth of newness, a joyful refreshment and sound of praise that recalibrates the day. We don't' need to wait for something big or small to happen, we can celebrate before something has happened by focusing on the vibrational resonance of joy.

3. What am I noticing?

This is about enhancing awareness and observation of both self and environment. It is a place of non-judgmental thought, a way to get in touch with what you are feeling. The key is observing rather than transforming. You are able to receive beyond the immediate demands and noise. By focusing your attention towards your intuitive centers, your gut, your feelings or heart, often you are often able to discern and sense far more than what your natural senses pick up. By placing your attention on these, it adds value to those senses and allows them to mature and become more in-tune over time.

Examples of this include:

Today I am noticing ... a difference between my intuition and my gut-feel centers. My intuition acts quickly and all the time whereas my gut-feel kicks in when something is either connected to my purpose in life or a warning system. My gut feel often pushes me to pray whereas my intuition is more just 'good to know' information.

Today I am noticing ... a sound of rushing water with a cool breeze blowing on my face. I feel as if there is a movement of water into the world. I also noticed a bitter taste in my mouth this usually happens when there is gossip happening about me.

At first what you are noticing might be more about yourself, but as time goes on it is possible to place the things you are noticing into a greater context. Sometimes it isn't an indication of your own emotion but rather a discernment of something that is happening globally.

4. Meditation

This journal is a meditation journal, so obviously meditation is a component. Perhaps you don't have time to meditate, in which case it could be a journal about a profound dream, or just a moment that you decide to journal. However, I have found it extremely useful to make note of the various types of meditation I choose to do on a specific day. Whether that is just breathing, repeating a specific name of God, repeating a Bible verse or saying specific Hebrew letters in different formations. If I experience a lot of God's presence during a specific meditation I can go back and repeat it. I can then figure out later if there is something about that meditation that resonates with who I am. If I meditate in a new way it is good to record that and be able to go back in the years to come and repeat that way of meditation. This is also a fun place to play around with your meditation practice. Where did you meditate, did you meditate in the full sunlight, or did you dim the lights and play soothing music? Does a specific environment or set of conditions, perhaps starting with worship or reading the Bible, enhance your meditation?

5. Spiritual Insight

Spiritual insight is the bulk of this journal and the main purpose for creating it. The purpose of this section is to write down what you experienced in meditation. We have created a set of prompts specifically for this section to remind you of things you might have experienced during your meditation and to increase your awareness of all your spiritual and physical senses. Please know that it is entirely ok if you saw nothing, felt nothing or encountered nothing. It might just be a reaffirmation of the knowledge that God loves you. It is also completely ok if all you write down is what you wondered in your mind while the meditation happened or if you saw light and then rationalized it - that is perfectly ok too. There are no rules to this. This is your journal, your senses and your thoughts. If nothing specific stood out this might be the space to consider the prompt questions at the beginning of each day.

For us personally, we have discovered that by writing these post meditation entries often, the seemingly small thing that catches the peripheral edge of our attention, such as a sense of weight behind a specific word, becomes significant in our growth with God and extremely important in the development of our awareness. By merely acknowledging the seemingly insignificant, it gives that perceiving sense the validation and confidence it needs to grow. It says, "this is valuable enough to draw my attention to."

By attributing value through attention to something that would otherwise be just a fleeting thought, forgotten not remembered, marks it with an exclamation point. This metaphorical exclamation mark forces us to pay more attention to that perceiving sense the next time it receives information, subsequently growing our daily awareness and spiritual/perceiving senses.

Examples of this section could include:

- Physical Sense (sight, sound, touch, taste, smell)
- Body awareness (tingling in hands, changes in heat, specific places in the body are connected with specific things, neurological architecture)
- Soul Senses (heart knowing, mind intuition, gut feeling)
- Behavior patterns, wounding,
- Spiritual Senses (Hebrew letters, angelic, dreams)

An entire list of spiritual insight prompts are included at the beginning of each section.

6. Manifestation

It is really important to both of us that our meditation is infused into our daily lives. That we are able to drive or focus the energy or essence that we gain from our intimate moments with God into something that shapes, changes or heals the world. One of the methods we use to continuously increase the awareness of God's presence in our lives throughout the day is visualization.

The cue to start this visualization is to describe the day ahead using the past tense, so that it feels as if it has already happened. So instead of I would like to do 'x, y or z'. you would say today I did 'x' and it was an incredible experience as it deepened my relationship with 'y' and created a sense of intimacy. While writing about the day ahead using past tense language, try and visualize each moment. Try and feel each feeling and how you feel at the end of your amazing day. Try engage as many of your senses as you can during this exercise.

The practice of visualizing the day or designing the day is multi-functional. It forces you to concretize your will, determine your priorities and organize your thoughts such that the day you create depicts this. It causes you to exercise your mental focus and forces you to spend time in the place of creating; creating a day and projecting it from your mind. It also helps shift that which you learnt or experienced in meditation from an "interesting piece of information," to something tangible that impacts your daily life. You are now no longer someone who generates energy through meditation but someone who directs it purposefully. If you decide to design your day creating space for the presence of God to inhabit, for miracles to occur and unusual opportunities, it will cause your internal awareness to increase its capacity to notice God at every turn and cause you to become aware of the inhabitation of God's presence throughout your daily life. Try it and see for yourself.

Is there a difference between Mercy and Compassion?

Gratitude
Today I am celebrating The goodness of life! The beauty of nature and the power of these waterfalls but how it is so important to take time to enjoy the cycle of rest and productivity. To allow rest and the beauty of this scenery to nourish my soul. Each waterfall Joseph and I have seen on this trip is more intriguing, more detailed and more exquisite than the one before. As deep cries out to deep in the roar of Your waterfalls. It is a privilege to experience the beauty of this world!

Self - Awareness
Today I am noticing An internal kind of holding of my breath; like something is being plotted or planned, something underhand or unexpected. Like something is brewing that perhaps has a negative aftertaste. The only word I can describe is a defensive stance. I have scanned Joseph and my life and it doesn't' seem connected to us; perhaps it is something brewing on the global stage. I will need to sit with God in meditation and see if there is something He desires of me or if this is just an awareness He desires me to cultivate. Mercy is the source and Compassion are the streams that flow from mercy but perhaps sometimes the act of what is truly merciful doesn't feel like a compassionate response? I need to think about this more.

Meditation
Did I follow through with my morning meditation ritual today ☑Y ☐N
Today was a long meditation but it was good. I felt it was important to shift my meditation to light and infusing the light of the Glory of Christ into all aspects. I did 4 aspects to meditation. I did some stretching with breath to release my shoulders and increase lung capacity, then purely breath, then alternate nostril breath to expand my capacity. After this I did a visualization of light with the 12 physiological systems and then I continued with my 10-minute chant, created a YHVH structure and began to focus all my attention to building light. After I felt saturated by the presence of God, I began to shift structures towards light and infuse every part of my self (local) family (regional)l and global with light. At which point I ended my meditation with a reflection type meditation moving to a position of unobscured gazing into the face and reflecting back the glory that is being projected by the face of God. The small face that gazes upon the big face and back again.

Spiritual Insight
During today's meditation I am sensed, saw, felt, learnt, experienced ...
Today I sensed the presence of a lot of angelic during my meditation especially during my mediation with the face. It took quite a while to drop down into the place where I could experience the radiance of the face unobscured. I think if I had not done all that pre-relaxation and saturation work, I would have struggled to have accessed that place of the face. I was initially surprised at

how much understanding, knowledge, emotion, thought, desire, intention and attention etc. was expressed through the radiating light. I guess that's where that verse that you would have the power to comprehend the love of Christ and to know this love that surpasses knowledge. That which was contained within the light was so full and dense. I think I need to go and do some research on the small or short face (Zeir Anpin) and see what others have experienced in this arena. The place I stood when encountering the small face almost felt like the foundation stone, it was that deeply embedded into the depths. There was some connection between the face and the angelic that deliver the radiance of His glory into creation. I will need to revisit this at a later date. Also, if there is a face, it must be attached to a head? What is behind the small face of God? What is that which exists in the mind of that face? Is the small face only a reflection of the big face? Or does it have a specific function?

I also felt when I was doing the wrapping of vitality with each physiological system that there was a lot of activity, blockage at 3 specific points in my physical body. Two of which were the interaction between my emotional soul and physical body, I acknowledged the trapped emotions thanked them and honored them and opened each point to receive the love of God so that, that tension could be released.

However, the third point felt like it wasn't connected to myself but again that global feeling that someone was shifting something on a bigger scale. Moving a global gate of some kind. I will return to that point and open it up in the presence of God during tomorrow's meditation but at the time I invited all the angels of wisdom and the spirit of wisdom and understanding to show me what this was about and why it is specifically connected to that part of my body?

Manifestation
Write about the day you want to have in past tense as if it has already happened.

Today I had an extremely productive day. I was able to build into my long-term goals while enjoying the delight and favor of God at every turn. I spent an hour reading the latest clinical journal articles of the mind and God provided many lightning flashes of what that would look like in practice, what the end results of each of these technology advances were moving towards. I began to grasp an image of medicine in the future and the capacity of the human brain. In addition to this I spent time in nature, just connecting with the beauty and allowing myself to rest in the constant rush of the waterfalls. I became aware of the presence of 2 specific angels connected to this beauty and I witnessed a rare natural phenomenon. The rest of the day I spent enjoying Joseph and God showed me a new way to celebrate him. My day was extremely intentional and each of the activities I felt saturated by the delight and love of God.

How do I motivate myself when I don't feel like doing anything?

Gratitude
Today I am celebrating   Vision, Provision and Action

Self - Awareness
Today I am noticing   A real lack of motivation, which would be why I am celebrating. As I celebrate, I remember the goodness of God where I have broken through before and as I allow myself to bathe in that goodness motivation, excitement and joy overtake me.

Meditation   ☑ N
Did I follow through with my morning meditation ritual today

Today's meditation was short, quick, to the point and used extraordinary amounts of energy in one direction. I did my declarations in a loud voice between every layer and it was effective.

Spiritual Insight
During today's meditation I am sensed, saw, felt, learnt, experienced ...

I saw myself breaking through into new areas that have been previously closed and ideas immediately flooded my thoughts as to how to accomplish it easily and quickly.

As the structure came into view, I went inside it and constructed it from bottom to top and then opened it so that it could begin to intersect with the declarations and what comes from above. As the names were locking in the dimensions opened and the angels were released to go an accomplish the declarations. The ideas that flooded my head came from my upper self who was standing in front of me, mirroring my movements within the structure. I was also aware of various angelic waiting for my command to go as directed.

Manifestation
Write about the day you want to have in past tense as if it has already happened.

I woke up this morning clear and rested with a clear view of what needed to happen. First, coffee. Then I began to research for the answers I needed. The answers came clearly and I pulled the right strings to make them happen. I finished by 3 and hit the golf course. Had fantastic encounters while on the course that brought clarity and breakthrough for those who are around me and then texted them that evening to let them know I had been engaging.

"God is the one who leads me and elevates me to that state. I do not go to it on my own, for by myself I would not know how to want, desire, or seek it. I am now continually in this state. Furthermore, God very often elevates me to this state with no need, even, for my consent; for when I hope or expect it least, when I am not thinking about anything, suddenly my soul is elevated by God and I hold dominion over and comprehend the whole world. It seems, then, as if I am no longer on earth but in heaven, in God."

Saint Angela of Foligno

PERSONAL PRACTICE AND OUR JOURNALING ADVENTURE

The practice of journaling always sort-of reminds me of the difference between a first glimpse versus a concentrated stare. The grooms first look at the bride can be overwhelming, a rush of emotions and a blinding of beauty that wells up in his heart. Similarly, that first glimpse at a sunrise seems almost too bright and glistening when it is seen from beneath sleepy eyes but it is the second look, the held gaze that causes you to slow down and absorb all the details, the pastel colors of the perpetual dawn, the radiant beauty of what is presented and even later when reflecting back on that moment it allows you to place that memory into its greater context in order to access its meaning. By choosing to revisit that moment it gives it value within the greater context of your life. This is the art of journaling and the beauty that is derived from reflection.

Journaling and the art of reflecting has taken various forms throughout my life. My initial decision to journal began in high school when I didn't want to forget the beauty I was experience in my relationship with God. It was a practice of remembrance, that turned into a practice of gratitude and expression of love for God. In university reflection was a critical part of developing clinical reasoning and improving the way, methods and efficiency of treatments for patients. Over time it has evolved from only a written method, to incorporate travel memoirs, impactful conversations and thought-provoking questions.

As an extremely 'outcomes focused' individual driven by contribution, sustaining creation and the advancement of humanity, the current role of journaling is to help me hold the phase "journey over destination," in the forefront of my mind so I don't trip over my own feet as I propel myself towards my desired destination. It is a constant reminder for me to enjoy the adventure of life, to dream expansively while taking deep breaths so that the current reality becomes equally delightful and satisfying. Journaling is one of the ways that helps me intensify my delight in the luminous path also called the journey.

In my relationship with Joseph, reflection and paying attention to the things that might have been considered seemingly unimportant has provided us with critical pieces of the puzzle and timely insight. We both take time to share and contemplate dreams, experiences and encounters. Through carefully constructed questions we have used the art of verbal reflection to grow in our relationship with God, with one another and we have come to increasingly rely on each other's questions as a way of accessing deeper layers of mystery that perhaps would not have been discovered if dismissed without any attention spotlighted on it.

It is our greatest hope that this journal will create within you an intentionality that causes your senses to become attuned and alert and attentive to both your spirit and soul, so that the hidden depths of beauty and delight that are positioned on the journey will become known to you.

PART 1:

THE RADIANT ILLUMINATED SOUL

The radiance of the mystical soul is beyond description and imagination. Few have even broached the topic of the billowing, glorified essence that flows seamlessly up and down its interconnected magnificence. Who is worthy to even begin to describe the perfection that has descended from above? Who knows the perfect design of the intellect and its woven-ness with divinity? How can it be that to even consider these things one must realize they know nothing yet cannot live another day without knowing all that was intended to be known? As one famous rabbi said, "He is the knowledge, the knower and the known." To contemplate these mysteries is both privilege and suffering as the end of a matter is the beginning of another. The beauty of divinity reflected in the soul may never be fully realized but there is no nobler pursuit than to fall in love with the process. This is the journey we are on and this is the journey we present to you; to discover the beauty hidden within and to fall in love with the Father of Light, with Jesus Christ and with the Person of Holy Spirit through the discovery of how you were formed and fashioned in his mind from Eternity.

LEARNING TO WRITE I AM STATEMENTS

What is an "I am statement"?

An "I am" statement is similar to a declaration but is linked to our identity which is rooted in Christ and continues to state the subsequent actions we take as a result of our identity in Christ. An "I am" statement is extremely powerful as the spiritual realm responds to who you are not what you do. The world has taught us that what we produce is of ultimate importance, however this is not true. Who we are, because of who Christ is (we are made righteous because He is righteous), is what the spirit world recognizes.

3 components of "I am" statements

For clarity, let's expand on this concept further. There are three main components to I am statements:

      a.) Our connection to the Great I am.

We begin with the name of God "I am" and apply it in the way Jesus demonstrated in the book of John. When we consider the words *"Ehyeh Asher Ehyeh"* in the most simplistic form it has two basic definitions and an application useful for our purposes. Firstly, it means: I am that I am. Secondly it means: I will be what I will be. Our basic application of this definition is that "I am already that which I will become." It is a statement about the future and the past contained within the present. It is an identity that removes time from the equation so that what is displayed in the present is the expression of provision that is needed for that specific occasion.

With this definition in mind, we can begin in John chapter 6 and move through the entire book of John looking at how Jesus framed what he demonstrated and demonstrated what he framed through "identity" statements.

- "I am the bread of life"
- "I am the way, truth and life"
- "I am the light of the world"
- "I am the resurrection"
- "I am the door"
- "I am the good shepherd"

When Jesus framed up his identity statement it always had to do with what he was demonstrating or doing or becoming at the time. Jesus became the embodiment of His identity statements in order to accomplish the miracles he performed. He became the provision that was needed in that specific circumstance.

b.) The action or provision that stems from the identity

Continuing to observe Jesus' statements, it is evident that the "I am" was just the first part of the statement. The second part was always an accompanying act or qualifier as to what the "I am" does. "I am the way, the truth and the life," is the identity statement. What does the "I am" do? In this case it is "no one comes to the father except through me". Let's observe another, "I am the bread of life." What does the "I am" do in this instance? "He who comes to me shall never hunger and he who believes in me shall never thirst." Jesus said this right after he performed a massive miracle having to do with food. You can trace almost every miracle Jesus did in the book of John to an identity statement where he pronounced who 'He' was and then demonstrated what the "who I am" does. He became the embodiment of resurrection in order to raise Lazarus from the dead.

c.) Solidifying our identity in Christ

Identity is paramount for the direction we are moving as a body. It is the platform we use to launch into higher realms of our destiny and to expand our influence as sons. It structures the environment around us to ensure we can operate as God desires and as we desire. It shapes the spiritual world around us and clothes our angelic help with raiment fitting for someone in our position. There is much to be said here, but for now we encourage you to begin to explore yourself the possibility of what God has provided. I will leave you with a few examples as we continue and encourage you to come up with your own:

I am	Which accomplishes
I am Love	it drips from every pore of my being and I use it to help bring the destiny of others forward
I am wisdom	I meet with her daily and successful global business drips from my fingers like honey
I am knowledge	I am fully proficient in the mysteries of heaven
I am a King	I speak and it is

Scope of Identity Statements

There is no limit to the arenas in which identity statements can be made: personal, family, career etc. Speaking out an identity statement like this at the end of your meditation time will thrust the angelic force around you into action bringing the needed resources and revelation towards you so that your identity launch pad can grow and your relationship with our Loving Father can deepen.

SPIRITUAL INSIGHT PROMPTS

1. Insight, Intuition and Revelation
- What revelation did I gain from the meditation?
- What new understanding did I receive?
- Did I feel like what I learnt was new understanding, or a remembrance?
- What creative or inspired thoughts did I have during my meditation?
- What wisdom or understanding did I gain through my meditation?
- How did my perspective about a situation change through my meditation?
- As a result of my meditation, did I feel like I was being prompted or gently moved to shift or change something in response to the love of God? Did I gain insight of something within myself that needed to change, grow, be discarded or developed?
- Was there something specific I identified during my meditation that I would like to take time to dig deeper into at a later stage?

2. Perception
- At any point during the meditation did I have a sensation of weightiness attached to a specific word, prayer, bible verse or thought?
- When I said the names of God, called on the blood of Jesus or engaged with the Holy Spirit, did I sense the weight of God behind my meditation?
- During my meditation did I gain an impression or perception of something outside of myself? Perhaps a sense of something in the atmosphere? Perhaps a sense of something at a global level?
- When I meditate can I perceive others in the atmosphere? Can I perceive the impact of the Church? Does it feel the same every day of the week? Do certain days in my area feel different? If there are multiple frequencies, can I separate them out and determine the strongest frequency, the weakest? Which one pulls towards me? Which one pushes away?

3. Spiritual Sight
- Where is Jesus in the midst of my meditation?
- How is the Holy Spirit present in my meditation?
- Did I see any angels or beings, people from the Cloud of Witnesses, aspects of the Holy Spirit or perhaps an aspect of creation from before the fall? A memory contained within the flame of God?
- Did you engage any people from the Cloud of Witnesses, rabbi's, priests, mystics of old; dignitaries, kings or noblemen; or specific people from your own genealogy?
- Did you encounter any ancient civilizations or cities, any original cultures or ever living ones?

Sense of Movement

- During my meditation did I see any flashing light? Was there any color? Is there as specific aspect of meditation that these lights are associated with?
- Did I see a flash of any specific images held in space?
- Am I able to re-engage anything I saw at a later time?
- Is there something that I always see in meditation that I take for granted as normal?
- Did I see something unusual in meditation that I do not understand but need to describe?
- Where is the grey area or area you cannot see into? Can I focus on it and move beyond the unknown and unseeable?

4. Feelings

- During my meditation did I perceive movement? Did I sense something walking past me? Walking into the room, or out of the room? Swirling, circling, spiraling movement?
- When I meditate on things beyond myself is there an area (spiritual, global, national) that I perceive movement within?
- Was there a predominant feeling I had during meditation? Does that feeling come from me and the things that are going on in my life? The atmosphere around me or something external (perhaps another person projecting their feelings, the Holy Spirit bringing a sense of peace and comfort?)
- During meditation was there something specific that made me feel more peaceful and relaxed? Safe?
- Did I at any stage during my meditation connect with the intense delight of God? What was it in relation to? Am I aware of the feelings of God? Delight? Exuberant joy? Compassion? Kindness?
- When I meditate on the names of God, do they elicit a specific feeling? When I encounter an angel, being or member of the Cloud of Witnesses or a specific letter of light, do I experience a specific feeling?
- When I feel something can I turn my heart towards it and see what it is or what is causing that feeling?
- How did I feel before meditating and how did I feel after meditating? Was there a change? How long does that feeling last after meditation is finished? Does it dissipate immediately? Do I carry throughout the day? Can I go back and access that feeling if I need refreshment and remembrance?

5. Auditory

- Can I hear sounds when I meditate? Inaudible or audible? Music or voices?
- The Psalms often talk about the sound associated with natural phenomena like the rushing waters, the galling wind, the crackling fire? Does the land I am standing on have a sound? Do I ever hear sound associated with thunder or other natural phenomena?

- Do I ever hear sound associated with movement? Crackling, whooshing?
- Is there a specific aspect of meditation or position/place I engage that is connected to a specific sound? Is that sound connected to healing? The throne? Angels singing? Is the music of the spheres present?
- Is the frequency I am hearing in one particular spot or does it pervade the atmosphere?
- Can I determine which direction the sounds are coming from? Do I only see and hear what is in front of me?
- What increases the sound? What decreases the sound? If you lean into your heart, does it increase the sound or does the sound of the waters of your heart muddy the sound you are hearing?
- Are there sounds associated with others people? Friends, family, loved ones?
- What about music connected to ancient cultures? Have I ever encountered these sounds? Or music associated with different geographical locations?

6. Olfactory and Taste

- When I meditate do I smell any fragrance at any point in my meditation? Is it sweet? Is it fruity? Is it plant like? Is it floral? Is it more ancient like old books and dusty? Is it medicinal like eucalyptus? Is it woodsy like fir or cedar? Or monastery-like, such as frankincense?
- When do the fragrances in my meditation occur? Often during moments of silent gratitude people have reported heighted sense of smell? Has that occurred for you?
- In my daily life do I ever experience or encounter a fragrance? Does that match or compliment the fragrances I encounter in my meditation?
- Do I ever experience a sweet or bitter taste during meditation?

7. Physical

- Where on my body am I feeling the presence of God? Was I acutely aware of any of my physical body parts? Perhaps my heart? My spine? My knees?
- Did I feel a sensation of heat, energy building or tingling at any point during the meditation? What was I engaging at that point in time?
- Different to energy heat, did I maybe feel a cool air or breeze? A watery liquid movement or a fiery burning heat sensation?
- What is my preferred meditation stance? Sitting, lying standing? Is there a difference when I cross my legs and arms? Is there a difference when I meditate with my hands facing upwards? Is there a difference when I place my hand on my heart?
- Am I aware of the energy that flows through my body? During my meditation was I aware of any blockages in the flow of energy? During my meditation was I aware of my breath passing easily throughout my body?
- Can I shift the place from which I breathe? Does that change what I am able to perceive or the type of things that I am perceiving?

- Feelings sometimes are reflected as colors at the level of the body when emotion is stored in a specific body part. When I meditate do I connect feelings and colors together? Do I see specific colors residing over specific parts of my body? Can I change the colors or intensify the colors that reside at different parts of my body?
- Am I aware of places in my physical body that function as spiritual gates? Am I aware of these gates? Do I sense when these gates are sealed? Are they connected to God? Other people?

Self -Awareness and Connection

- During my meditation did I feel a strengthening of my connection to God, to the life of Christ and the hope of Christ within me? If I did communion during meditation, did I experience a sense of connection to the depth of Christ's love contained within the blood of Jesus and the voice of the blood of Jesus that speaks for us?
- Did I experience a connecting to the wisdom of God or the understanding, the mercy or the strength of God? An increased sense of confidence and inner strength resulting from my connection to Christ? (I can do all things through Christ who strengthens me).
- In my meditation did I feel an increase, build up or boost of love, life and light of God growing within me and expanding outwards? Did I feel refreshed through my meditation?
- Did my meditation increase my awareness of the unique beauty I bring to creation? A specific aspect of myself or my identity? Did it establish anything specific in my life?
- Has my meditation increased my awareness of my own voice and sound within creation?

Moving forward

- How do I honor that which I have seen, heard, smelled, tasted, felt or perceived during my meditation? Do I dismiss it as fantasy and throw it away? Do I bring it to Jesus and allow it to be held in a place of love and connection?
- What aspects of my meditation do I need to revisit? Take with me into the next meditation? It could be a specific meditation technique that elicited an insight or it could be an insight that needs to be focused on to drive it further.

UNIQUE AND EXQUISITE CREATION

You are the most unique and exquisite being in creation. Without equal, you stand as the pinnacle of God's handiwork. The supreme creation of the omnipotent creator born in the depths of his mind, carrying the full attention of His Heart. This loving Father and His son Jesus Christ have set not only a precedent for identifying yourself but also a standard and an example. When the question of "Who are you?" inevitably comes, there is but one answer. I am. For the purposes of illustration, and so that it will stick in your mind, the follow up is "What am you?" The answer to that question is not only the action of the identity but the boundary lines through which your life will be guided.

Who does Jesus identify with in His statements? Who are you? What does the Bible say about you and what do you do with it? This week the theme we would like to introduce as part of your meditation is this: "You are a unique and exquisite creation." I am unique and exquisite, new dimensions of the Love of God are constantly being revealed to me.

We have provided the "I am" part for this week, you fill in the rest. What direction do you want your life to take? What aspects of God do you want to grow in? Where do you want to go in your own secret place with God? These statements become the keys that unlock the door to intimacy that is dreamed about yet rarely gained. Your identity will become the platform you launch from to reach the depths of God. Most people want this but few know how to or are willing to pay the price to grow towards it. May your mind be blown and your hand be ready to write.

Identity Statement

I am...

which accomplishes (associated action)

DAY	FOCUS POINT	MEDITATION PLAN
SUNDAY		
MONDAY		
TUESDAY		
WEDNESDAY		
THURSDAY		
FRIDAY		
SATURDAY		

Notes

When was the last I time I showed up in the fullness of who I am? What did that look like? What did that feel like? What stirred me to show up like that?

Gratitude
Today I am celebrating

Self - Awareness
Today I am noticing

Meditation
Did I follow through with my morning meditation ritual today   [Y] [N]

Spiritual Insight
During today's meditation I am sensed, saw, felt, learnt, experienced ...

Manifestation
Write about the day you want to have in past tense as if it has already happened.

Sketch Space

Who is the type of person that could get the results or outcomes that I want in my life? What does that person look like? What do their daily habits entail? What of their character traits, routines or activities do I need to develop to become the type of person that achieves the results I want?

Gratitude
Today I am celebrating

Self - Awareness
Today I am noticing

Meditation
Did I follow through with my morning meditation ritual today   Y N

Spiritual Insight
During today's meditation I am sensed, saw, felt, learnt, experienced ...

Manifestation
Write about the day you want to have in past tense as if it has already happened.

Sketch Space

What is an outrageous or bold aspect of my identity that I want to claim or develop? Dig deep, this might stem from a desire or dream that I am too afraid to voice?

Gratitude
Today I am celebrating

Self - Awareness
Today I am noticing

Meditation
Did I follow through with my morning meditation ritual today Y N

Spiritual Insight
During today's meditation I am sensed, saw, felt, learnt, experienced ...

Manifestation

Write about the day you want to have in past tense as if it has already happened.

Sketch Space

The environment around us often becomes a mirror to the beliefs, thought and feelings we project from our inner world. Are there beliefs about my identity that I can identify that are being reflected back to me from my current situation/life/ environment?

Gratitude
Today I am celebrating

Self - Awareness
Today I am noticing

Meditation   Y N
Did I follow through with my morning meditation ritual today

Spiritual Insight
During today's meditation I am sensed, saw, felt, learnt, experienced ...

Manifestation
Write about the day you want to have in past tense as if it has already happened.

Sketch Space

Embodying my true identity takes time and work. What are some of the practices that I currently do or want to do that help me embrace my core self? This could be mentally (visualization/reading), spiritually (declarations/meditation), emotionally and physically.

Gratitude
Today I am celebrating

Self - Awareness
Today I am noticing

Meditation   Y N
Did I follow through with my morning meditation ritual today

Spiritual Insight
During today's meditation I am sensed, saw, felt, learnt, experienced ...

Manifestation

Write about the day you want to have in past tense as if it has already happened.

Sketch Space

How do I honor the unique creation that I am, the identity that is forged within me, the person that I am? (This could be actions such as settings boundaries, it could be nurturing a specific aspect of yourself?)

Gratitude
Today I am celebrating

Self - Awareness
Today I am noticing

Meditation
Did I follow through with my morning meditation ritual today   Y N

Spiritual Insight
During today's meditation I am sensed, saw, felt, learnt, experienced ...

Manifestation

Write about the day you want to have in past tense as if it has already happened.

Sketch Space

DATE & PLACE:

What beliefs about myself do I need to upgrade in order to be who I desire to be?
Can I create an I am statement to solidify my new formed belief? How do these new
aspects of identity inform my actions?

Gratitude
Today I am celebrating

Self - Awareness
Today I am noticing

Meditation   Y N
Did I follow through with my morning meditation ritual today

Spiritual Insight
During today's meditation I am sensed, saw, felt, learnt, experienced …

Manifestation

Write about the day you want to have in past tense as if it has already happened.

Sketch Space

THE SOUL OF MAN SET ABLAZE BY THE FLAME OF GOD

You are impossibly interconnected with Divinity. So much so that it is "impossible to escape His love." Situated perfectly in the back of your head is the seat of your spirit. Concealed in this holy space is the mystery of the entanglement between you and Christ. It is the place where your spirit and His spirit have become one spirit and also the place where your mind (intellect) and His connect. This Yechida flame is the "light that shines" and the "Candle of the Lord." It is this light that causes the lavish radiant energies of the soul that burst forth like glittering paint colors, creating an almost poetic and inspirational brilliance to an otherwise void existence. Evoking the senses and pushing them beyond the outward appearance of man's mundane daily interactions, transmuting them into receptive perceiving devices able to reach into the essence of what lies beneath, the hidden beauty.

It is the soul of man, saved by Christ, valued by God as a prized treasure that becomes saturated and drips with the luminous light of Christ, enlivened by the flame of God. It is the mind of this new creation man that becomes brilliant in its ability to infuse its creations and innovations with the capacity to produce life. Each thought and seed that is planted from the city of the light infused mind becomes a beacon on the hill of creation, causing those that pass by to experience the glimmering rays of hope. Christ in us the hope of glory (Col 1:27). The good Samaritan of innovation, science, engineering and thoughtful genius that steers the compassion and love of God towards all of humanity. Such is the saturated intellect of the soul.

Now the illuminating flame moves beyond the enlightened mind to the radiant waters of the heart of God's beloved and begins to reflect like a diamond; the full spectrum of rainbow colors. This is the place where the seeds of the mind are planted and bound with the purity of the heart's intent. This is the place where the desires of the heart and thoughts of the mind unite. When these seeds of life are wrapped with light such that the emotions of the soul dance upon the radiant waters dazzling the mundane and adding a reflective quality to the body. The uplifted soul that embraces the movement of light and the dance of light produces an array of light that penetrates the inner being of God himself and has no imaginable equal. The fragrances of eternity born from the heart of man are thrust into the domain of the Holy One.

The seed moves from the enlightened mind to the radiant waters of the heart of God's beloved and reflects like a diamond the full spectrum of rainbow colors. This is the place where seeds are bound with the purity of the heart's intent and emotions that dazzle the mundane and add reflective quality to the body. You are not just another mystic; you are the enwrapped desire of divinity.

This week the meditation is simple. We are celebrating the beautiful radiant soul of man infused by the flame of God.

Joseph C Sturgeon II

Identity Statement

I am...

which accomplishes (associated action)

DAY	FOCUS POINT	MEDITATION PLAN
SUNDAY		
MONDAY		
TUESDAY		
WEDNESDAY		
THURSDAY		
FRIDAY		
SATURDAY		

Notes

DATE & PLACE:

While peering into the mystery of your interconnection and intertwining with Christ, contemplating no separation from the love of God (Romans 8), staring into the flame of love from which my spirit was cut, consider what is available in this flame? What is the hope of glory?

Gratitude
Today I am celebrating

Self - Awareness
Today I am noticing

Meditation
Did I follow through with my morning meditation ritual today

Y N

Spiritual Insight
During today's meditation I am sensed, saw, felt, learnt, experienced ...

Manifestation

Write about the day you want to have in past tense as if it has already happened.

Sketch Space

Imagine I am a righteous oak tree in a vast expanse. A fire reaches down from heaven, starting at the back of my head, the tallest branch working its way down the entire tree until the whole tree is set ablaze by the fire of God. What does it mean for me personally to be set ablaze, exuding life and radiant light from every pore of my being?

Gratitude
Today I am celebrating

Self - Awareness
Today I am noticing

Meditation
Y N

Did I follow through with my morning meditation ritual today

Spiritual Insight
During today's meditation I am sensed, saw, felt, learnt, experienced ...

Manifestation
Write about the day you want to have in past tense as if it has already happened.

Sketch Space

What does it mean to be a new creation, something completely different from what was made before? Not an upgraded version but a man comprising not only of body and soul - but body, soul and spirit? What does the "old has gone the new has come," mean for all aspects of my life? What patterns of behaviors, thought and beliefs change as I embrace my identity as a new man, inseparable from the love of God?

Gratitude
Today I am celebrating

Self - Awareness
Today I am noticing

Meditation
Did I follow through with my morning meditation ritual today

Y N

Spiritual Insight
During today's meditation I am sensed, saw, felt, learnt, experienced ...

Manifestation

Write about the day you want to have in past tense as if it has already happened.

Sketch Space

The soul is comprised of 5 aspects. What does that mean for my 'mind' and 'heart' components of my soul to be saturated and set ablaze by abundant, full, richness of the life of Christ and the flame of God?

Gratitude
Today I am celebrating

Self - Awareness
Today I am noticing

Meditation
Did I follow through with my morning meditation ritual today [Y] [N]

Spiritual Insight
During today's meditation I am sensed, saw, felt, learnt, experienced ...

Manifestation

Write about the day you want to have in past tense as if it has already happened.

Sketch Space

What does that mean for the 'intuitive', 'physical/instinctual' and 'creative/sexual/productive' components of my soul to be saturated by the abundant, full, richness of the life of Christ and set ablaze by the flame of God?

Gratitude
Today I am celebrating

Self - Awareness
Today I am noticing

Meditation
Y N

Did I follow through with my morning meditation ritual today

Spiritual Insight
During today's meditation I am sensed, saw, felt, learnt, experienced ...

Manifestation

Write about the day you want to have in past tense as if it has already happened.

Sketch Space

Consider the phrase "enwrapped desire of divinity?" What does that mean for me personally to be the enwrapped desire of divinity? What does that feel like? Do any parts feel resistant to this kind of love? What response does this evoke in me? Does the knowledge of this kind of love impact my current identity?

Gratitude
Today I am celebrating

Self - Awareness
Today I am noticing

Meditation
Did I follow through with my morning meditation ritual today

Y N

Spiritual Insight
During today's meditation I am sensed, saw, felt, learnt, experienced ...

Manifestation

Write about the day you want to have in past tense as if it has already happened.

Sketch Space

DATE & PLACE:

After spending a week gazing upon the mystery of the divine entanglement between myself and Christ, reflecting on each aspect of my soul and looking into the depth of love that is consistently infusing my being, what response does this evoke towards God? What action, what feelings or desires does this understanding of love bring up within me?

Gratitude
Today I am celebrating

Self - Awareness
Today I am noticing

Meditation   Y N
Did I follow through with my morning meditation ritual today

Spiritual Insight
During today's meditation I am sensed, saw, felt, learnt, experienced …

Manifestation

Write about the day you want to have in past tense as if it has already happened.

Sketch Space

HARMONIZING MY INNER WORLD TO EXPAND MY ESSENCE AND INCREASE MY IMPACT

The energy systems of your soul are the manifestation implements within creation specifically purposed for you. Every individual has a different mix dependent upon your will, environment and a host of other conditions and choices. Every person on the face of the Earth has a choice as to how the energies move together and which ones are in control. Meditation is fantastic tool to begin to harmonize the energies of the soul and will aid you greatly in beginning to not only understand yourself in a more complete way but also begin to shift the atmosphere in your immediate surroundings.

The harmony of your soul is key to many areas of your life. This aspect can be deeply spiritual or not spiritual at all. For instance, one of the greatest gifts of harmonized soul energy is general happiness. People who have learned to balance the energy or who are naturally geared towards more balanced energy have a, generally speaking, happier life. Even in the midst of hardship there are no severe ups or downs, rage or depression, sexual impropriety, or mistakes that are commonly associated with difficult times. Having harmonized energy leads to better and more effective decision making and also gives a platform for the individual to move in many directions.

Most people who accomplish a lot in their lives are not "balanced" people. They are generally exceptions to every rule and move in extreme directions often. This leads to all kinds of breakthroughs and all kinds of problems at the same time. Being harmonized in the energy of your soul allows you to start and return to the balanced place. It is not to say that you are balanced at all times. More accurately said, one who can harmonize the energy of their soul effectively can also move in and out of extremes effectively depending upon the situation and the need.

The most important aspect of harmonizing energy for the soul is the will. Your will is the rudder to your spiritual ship, it is the key that accompanies love and through passion and desire unlocks your destiny. Claire and I spend extensive amounts of time exercising our will over the energies of our soul. It is a discipline in what the book of Galatians calls "Self Control." Mastery of this aspect of your life will perpetually grow into a greater impact within your sphere of influence.

Identity Statement

I am...

which accomplishes (associated action)

DAY	FOCUS POINT	MEDITATION PLAN
SUNDAY		
MONDAY		
TUESDAY		
WEDNESDAY		
THURSDAY		
FRIDAY		
SATURDAY		

Notes

What does the essence of who you are feel like? What does it produce? What makes the essence of your soul expand or be felt more powerfully? What makes it shrink and become less impactful?

Gratitude
Today I am celebrating
_____

Self - Awareness
Today I am noticing
_____
_____
_____
_____

Meditation   Y N
Did I follow through with my morning meditation ritual today
_____
_____
_____
_____

Spiritual Insight
During today's meditation I am sensed, saw, felt, learnt, experienced ...
_____
_____
_____
_____
_____
_____
_____
_____

Manifestation

Write about the day you want to have in past tense as if it has already happened.

Sketch Space

DATE & PLACE:

The essence of the soul is that which exists beneath all the layers of preference and bias that have been placed on top of it. How do the things I have called interests, likes and dislikes, personality etc. obscure the essence of my soul?
Are my identity statements rooted in my personality or are they rooted in the core essence of who I am?

Gratitude
Today I am celebrating

Self - Awareness
Today I am noticing

Meditation   Y N
Did I follow through with my morning meditation ritual today

Spiritual Insight
During today's meditation I am sensed, saw, felt, learnt, experienced ...

Manifestation

Write about the day you want to have in past tense as if it has already happened.

Sketch Space

DATE & PLACE:

Considering the 5 aspects of the soul that make up my essence (intellectual, intuition, emotional, physical or sexual/creative) which is the most predominant aspect of my soul? Which aspect do I use to modulate other aspects? (For instance, going for a run when I feel emotional would be using physical aspect to modulate the emotional component.)

Gratitude
Today I am celebrating

Self - Awareness
Today I am noticing

Meditation
Y N
Did I follow through with my morning meditation ritual today

Spiritual Insight
During today's meditation I am sensed, saw, felt, learnt, experienced ...

Manifestation

Write about the day you want to have in past tense as if it has already happened.

Sketch Space

How do I cultivate and grow or mature my soul? Is it something I actively pursue or is it something that is driven by external circumstances? What set of "rules" or conditions determine if I am going to endure something to benefit my soul or use spiritual techniques to remove it from my life?

Gratitude
Today I am celebrating

Self - Awareness
Today I am noticing

Meditation
Did I follow through with my morning meditation ritual today Y N

Spiritual Insight
During today's meditation I am sensed, saw, felt, learnt, experienced ...

Manifestation

Write about the day you want to have in past tense as if it has already happened.

Sketch Space

Do I notice flashes of insight in my mind that I receive from God? Do I forget most of my insight? Does my insight replicate my own perspective and personal bias or is it from something outside of myself?

Gratitude
Today I am celebrating

Self - Awareness
Today I am noticing

Meditation
Did I follow through with my morning meditation ritual today Y N

Spiritual Insight
During today's meditation I am sensed, saw, felt, learnt, experienced ...

Manifestation
Write about the day you want to have in past tense as if it has already happened.

Sketch Space

Do the waters and emotions of my soul bring me peace and refreshment? Do I enjoy my emotions or despise them? Do they cause me to feel thrown out of balance? How can I use breath to calm the waters of my soul?

Gratitude
Today I am celebrating

Self - Awareness
Today I am noticing

Meditation
Did I follow through with my morning meditation ritual today

Y N

Spiritual Insight
During today's meditation I am sensed, saw, felt, learnt, experienced …

Manifestation
Write about the day you want to have in past tense as if it has already happened.

Sketch Space

DATE & PLACE:

The soul is often likened to a painting, with many colors and no two souls are the same. Take a moment to consider the beauty of the soul and its expression. Perhaps there is a grateful delight in the uniqueness of my own soul that I desire to sit in and share with God. Perhaps it is the soul of family members, friends, colleagues or even the macro-perspective of the beauty of man within creation. Whatever the painting is that you wish to consider, take a moment to enjoy it with God.

Gratitude
Today I am celebrating

Self - Awareness
Today I am noticing

Meditation
Y N

Did I follow through with my morning meditation ritual today

Spiritual Insight
During today's meditation I am sensed, saw, felt, learnt, experienced ...

Manifestation
Write about the day you want to have in past tense as if it has already happened.

Sketch Space

THE PURPOSE OF MY LIFE

"If they ever tell my story, let them say I walked with giants. Men rise and fall like the winter wheat but these names will never die." Troy (the movie)

Every human life has a purpose or destiny, a way of contributing to the forward progression of humanity. It is so fundamental to our being that it makes up one of the four basic questions of human life. Why am I here? What is my purpose? Many people will ask this very question again and again at various conjunctions in their life. Depending on the phase in life, the question might look different? During high school this question is asked in relation to career? When considering one's theology it is asked as a means to related to the will of God, prayer and decision making. At the end of one's life it could be asked as a means of understanding personal significance? But the question remains; what is my purpose and what is my destiny?

Some of the most successful books, movies, computer games etc are founded around this question in something that is called the hero's journey. It is a framework comprising of 12 steps that map out the journey of the hero towards his destiny, and because it deals with his struggles on the journey not just in overcoming but also in accepting his call to destiny, it resonates with something deep inside. The Lord of the Rings is a great example of the hero's journey. In these stories the specifics of the journey and sometimes the specifics of the destiny are rarely known at the beginning of the quest. Perhaps this is because if we knew everything from the outset about the road we would need to walk through, we would become overwhelmed and would never set off on our quest.

Now it is fairly obvious that not all destinies are the same and as such their impact is not the same. Consider the births that occurred in the Bible where the Angel of the Lord was present. Each of the lives of those children drastically changed the course of history. However, there is something to be said about the magnetic call to something, whether that is the Angel of the Lord marking your life or an internal knowledge of identity that is constantly propelling you forward towards an inexplicable and even intangible outcome with increasing magnetism. There is something about a person whose will and purpose are aligned such that their purpose resounds throughout the entirety of their being causing every cell to resonate with the knowledge of who they are and what they will contribute to humanity with their life. Departing from delusions of grandeur, these individuals are not easily distracted and after grappling with who they are and this call towards their purpose. They are able to reach into the recesses of who they are and access the deepest reserves of their being such that they can persevere throughout the journey to fulfill their purpose and destiny,

And so it is from this place that we depart and begin to contemplate, meditate and tune our ear towards the call that God has placed on each of our lives. To explore the multispectral rays of the Lord's will and the endless possibility of what that could tangibly look like in your specific life.

Identity Statement

I am...

....

....

which accomplishes (associated action)

....

....

....

DAY	FOCUS POINT	MEDITATION PLAN
SUNDAY		
MONDAY		
TUESDAY		
WEDNESDAY		
THURSDAY		
FRIDAY		
SATURDAY		

Notes

....

....

....

Who is someone that inspires me or someone I admire? What is it about that person that inspires me? What qualities do I see in them that I desire to develop in my own life?

Gratitude
Today I am celebrating

Self - Awareness
Today I am noticing

Meditation
Did I follow through with my morning meditation ritual today   Y N

Spiritual Insight
During today's meditation I am sensed, saw, felt, learnt, experienced ...

Manifestation
Write about the day you want to have in past tense as if it has already happened.

Sketch Space

SEEING THROUGH WALLS   89

DATE & PLACE:

Do I consider destiny something that is fixed at birth, predetermined or something that can be changed? Can the righteous determine their own scroll or adventure or destiny?

Gratitude
Today I am celebrating

Self - Awareness
Today I am noticing

Meditation
Did I follow through with my morning meditation ritual today Y N

Spiritual Insight
During today's meditation I am sensed, saw, felt, learnt, experienced ...

Manifestation

Write about the day you want to have in past tense as if it has already happened.

Sketch Space

How important is the call to a destiny? Does it need to be God's audible or visible voice that calls me to my destiny? Is it an inward knowing or perhaps this is what I desire?

Gratitude
Today I am celebrating

Self - Awareness
Today I am noticing

Meditation
Y N

Did I follow through with my morning meditation ritual today

Spiritual Insight
During today's meditation I am sensed, saw, felt, learnt, experienced ...

Manifestation

Write about the day you want to have in past tense as if it has already happened.

Sketch Space

How do I perceive the will of God? Is it similar to a movie where every small decision impacts the destiny and needs to be brought before God? Is it more a matter of who I am, as His son, arranges the path?

Gratitude
Today I am celebrating

Self - Awareness
Today I am noticing

Meditation
Did I follow through with my morning meditation ritual today

Y N

Spiritual Insight
During today's meditation I am sensed, saw, felt, learnt, experienced ...

Manifestation

Write about the day you want to have in past tense as if it has already happened.

Sketch Space

What is an arena or area of interest that I can get lost in for hours? Reading books?
Talking and never losing interest? Why do I feel like this about this area?

Gratitude
Today I am celebrating

Self - Awareness
Today I am noticing

Meditation
Did I follow through with my morning meditation ritual today   Y N

Spiritual Insight
During today's meditation I am sensed, saw, felt, learnt, experienced ...

Manifestation

Write about the day you want to have in past tense as if it has already happened.

Sketch Space

Is compassion and calling the same thing? What are the areas that stir up a sense of passionate outrage or sense of injustice? Are these feelings provoked from a point of moral compassion for humanity or magnetic attraction to your destiny?

Gratitude
Today I am celebrating

Self - Awareness
Today I am noticing

Meditation
Did I follow through with my morning meditation ritual today ☐Y ☐N

Spiritual Insight
During today's meditation I am sensed, saw, felt, learnt, experienced ...

Manifestation

Write about the day you want to have in past tense as if it has already happened.

Sketch Space

DATE & PLACE:

What does "destined for greatness" look like for you? What would that look like in your own life? How does who you are connect to affect your destiny or life's purpose?

Gratitude
Today I am celebrating

Self - Awareness
Today I am noticing

Meditation
Did I follow through with my morning meditation ritual today

Y N

Spiritual Insight
During today's meditation I am sensed, saw, felt, learnt, experienced ...

Manifestation

Write about the day you want to have in past tense as if it has already happened.

Sketch Space

ADDITIONAL PROMPTS

Week 1: Identity
- What is the difference between identity that is rooted in personality vs identity that is rooted in who I am in Christ/ essence?
- Are there aspects of my life that I feel my identity is rooted in exterior things, such as crisis?
- Who does Jesus say I am? What do I look like in the Spirit? If I could summarise my core essence or values into 7 phrases, what would they be?
- What of my identity based on the roles I play? Mother, father, king/queen, son etc.?
- What happens in the spirit when I stand in the fullness of who I am in Christ? What is the impact of my words, actions in that place?
- What is the interaction between my identity and the Angel of the Faces?
- How do I clear the things that obscure this interaction/ reflection?
- How do the angels around my life respond when I function from my personality, as opposed to my identity?
- Write identity statements for your personal life, your spiritual life, your business or career and your family life.

Week 2 and 3: The Soul

General Soul and Celebrating the Soul
- How do you increase the infusion of the presence of God and the saturation of His light throughout your soul?
- What brings my soul delight? What brings it satisfaction? What causes it to become exuberant and alive?
- If time and money were no object, what experiences would your soul crave?
- Create an identity statement about the value of your soul.
- Ephesians 4:11 describes 5 energy systems: the apostle, the prophet, the evangelist, the teacher and the pastor. Another way of viewing these is the visionary, the strategist, the multiplier, the trainer and the nurturer. Yet another way these have been described is the generator, the manifestor, the reflector, the builder and the projector. Which of these descriptions best depicts you? Which functions do you find the easiest? Which do you find the hardest? How can you train all these aspects in your life?

Maturing the Soul
- What does a mature soul look like? What does MY mature soul look like?
- How does it react? How does it respond in uncomfortable situations?
- What practices or exercises do I do to help mature my soul or do I wait for external circumstances to force the soul to mature?
- What measures do I use to track the progress of my soul?

Joseph C Sturgeon II

- What can my mature soul do? Consider all the crazy sci-fi and fantasy movies, the trans-relocation, the time travel, the sky is the limit. Using the fullness of my imagination, try to picture what soul maturity could look like and could do.
- Is there a difference between an immature soul and a hurt soul?
- Who is someone who I would consider to be a mature soul? What does this look like in their life? What did they have to walk through in order for their soul to be mature? What was the cost of maturity?

Intellectual Awareness
- What does a focused mind and steadfast immoveable will look like? What does it look like within my own life?
- What daily practices do I do to train my mind and my focus and fix my attention?
- How does my meditation improve this?
- What is the difference between mechanical thought processes and inspired thinking infused by light? Can I identify areas in my life where I have formed mechanic mindsets opposed to growth mindsets?
- Am I aware of areas in my thinking where sentimentality overrides truth? Where my perspective is shaped by my bias, personality, likes and dislikes and sentimental attachments? How does this limit my interpretations, revelations and understanding?
- Thinking is considered a language; an internal dialogue. How does my internal dialogue influence who I am? What I believe I am capable of? And the love I believe I am able to receive from God?
- Listening requires the involvement of the intellect. How does listening to the word of God change my thinking?

Emotional Awareness
- Can I tell the difference between higher emotions that lead to transformation and lower emotions that push me to base survival mode?
- Can I discern the source of my feelings? Is it from the body such as tiredness, hunger etc. Is it from internal heart/soul movement or is it something in the external environment that I am picking up on? Can I determine what is stirring the waters of my soul? Where is the wind or the disturbance coming from?
- Consider each of the following emotional pairs:
  Anger and joy / peace; frustration and satisfaction; bitterness (depletion) and success; disappointment and surprise. How do I experience the tension of the negative emotion and the resolution of the positive emotion in my daily life? Is one of these pairs more dominant? Is one the root and the other a symptom? How do I use my emotions to increase my experience of life? The spirit realm? The relationships I have?
- Can I use my emotions to heap love and goodness and abundant life onto those around me? Can I use my emotions to be a wellspring of life, a bubbling fountain of refreshment?

- Transmuting Feelings: How do I take something that feels bad and transmute it? How do I take something that feels good and use it as a springboard into more?
- Do I feel something because I think with my mind that is how I ought to feel and believe it is the logical feeling attached to the experience, or do I genuinely feel something as a result of the movement of the waters within my heart?
- What is the connection between the meaning I assign to something and the emotions that I feel as a result of that assigned meaning?
- Colors have been associated with feelings. When meditating, do I see or perceive color? Connected to myself? Connected to others? Are those colors associated with specific body parts or feelings? Do those colors change? What causes them to change?

Perceived childhood and emotional soul wounds:

A summary of perceived childhood wounds are as follows: Self judgement, self- sacrifice, rejection of core self (worthy), rejection of identity (stems from a sense of not being seen and not being the same as. This wound results in a constant search for identity that will remove an innate feeling of loneliness and melancholy), rejection of intimacy, rejection of trust (safety issues), absence of nurturing (therefore need to nurture self, as no one will look after their needs), rejection of childhood (issues related to survival and strength), rejection of voice (participation in the world is unimportant, your voice or unique aspect is not important). These can result in questions related to "Does anyone see me? Does anyone hear me? Does anyone love me or value me?" Can I identity areas in my life where these questions are being raised? How does the Holy Spirit and the Father become the parent that reassures me of my value? How does Jesus become my inner child that replaces all childhood wounds?

Rest, Balance and Harmony

- What do I do for myself that enables me to show up in the fullness of who I am and for the people in my life?
- What things do I need to let go of, in order to move forward without being weighed down?

Week 4: Destiny and Purpose

Destination (questions for the wanderer)

- Rank the following broad topics in terms of importance in your ability to feel fulfilled or satisfied in life: Experiences (relationships, adventures, travel, encounters with God), Growth (health, intellect, skills, spiritual, maturing your soul, counselling etc.) and Contribution (career, creative life, community, impact, NGOs or causes, family life). How important is contribution to the makeup of who I am?
- Do I believe that my life has the capacity to change the world? How would that occur tangibly? What would that entail?

- What story do I want my life to tell and what roads do I need to choose in order for it to tell that story?
- What are some of the dreams and desires that terrify me because of how big they are? Can I identify any limiting beliefs that limit my capacity to dream?
- What are my typical excuses for not pursuing something life changing?
- What are the drivers that cause me to show up in the fullness of who I am? And what do these drivers tell me about myself? My destiny?
- What do I consider the most useful industry in the world? Why?
- What arenas do I feel most passionate about? What stirs my heart more than anything else? Is it sentimentality or is it a clue as to something I desire to change?
- For those who are journey focused, what goals have I set that have been accomplished so far? Maybe start by setting some short and medium term?
- What is an industry, skill or an area that I would be prepared to sacrifice at a high level for over a period of time in order to radically change this arena?
- What does Tikkun Olam (restoring the Earth) look like in the context of my life?
- For those who are journey focused, what daily tasks, meditations or practices have I created in order to keep me focused on the destination?

Journey (Questions for the determined)

- How do I celebrate the path and not only the destination? How do I express gratitude for the daily and not just push towards the overall?
- What are some things that inspire me to continue moving forward when I don't feel like it? (Favorite quotes, people's life stories or inspiring music etc).
- For those who are destination focused, what reminders have I placed around me which are clearly visible with my physical eyes that remind me to enjoy the journey?
- For those who are destination focused, what hobbies have I enjoyed this week that make me feel like the journey is worth it?

Immortality

- What skillset do you have or want to grow in that you believe will continue to add value to the world in 1000 years' time?
- How will I contribute to the generation that will be alive in 1500 years (other than some epic stories?)
- How can I interact with wisdom in a way that will serve me and my children well over the next 100 years?
- What is my 300-year plan?
- How have I identified with Jesus' Death, Burial, Resurrection and Ascension other than knowing a few bible verses? How have I engaged it in meditation?

THE SUBSTANCE OF YOUR NAME

There is an importance to a name that transcends time and space. Somehow, in His wisdom, God himself decided that naming something and someone would connect it or him to something much greater than himself as well as something unknown. Why is it that one of the promises in the book of Revelation to those who overcome is a new name? Naming has captivated the world. Look at the secret pass codes to get into to special places, look at the continuation of generations with the II, III, IV (we know someone who is a V). Look at Jr. and Sr. There are women in the world named after their mother, sons after fathers, and even dogs after favorite movie characters. What is in a name that even the names of God Himself are the passkeys, portal openers and star-gates to different dimensions. How can the name of a bible character be so connected to his calling that it pre-determines a giant portion of what he does? Pay special attention to the name of Jesus, why those letters, why in that order, what does it represent? The importance of a name cannot be overstated to the extent that even the most boring, general thing you have ever learned or been told can carry significant weight. Who are you? Where did you come from? What is your name? What does your name mean?

Can you identify how the meaning of your name could be included in an aspect of your destiny/purpose/who you are?

Behind the name of every nobleman, king, warrior or hero is the substance of who he is. That unfolding substance of character and essence that adds weight to the words that he says, strength to the action he takes and a trustworthiness to the outcome that is produced. It is this substance of character that enabled businessmen to trust deals made from mere handshakes, or conversely the predictability of character that creates fear and distrust around specific negotiations with untrustworthy opponents.

It is impossible to discuss identity, the soul and destiny without discussing the substance behind the name. The character and essence that one adds to the weight of one's signature, to the impact of their handshake and to the command of their words.

What are 5 specific character traits that you would like to be synonymous with your name? (The values, beliefs, principles, ideals that define you).

How do you intend to grow these aspects of character? What actions can you take to grow these aspects of character? Can you identify people in your life with these character traits? What does it feel like when you are around them? How do you honor those character traits when you see they are present in other's lives?

Create an "I am" statement that helps you embody these characteristics

What check-in questions can you ask yourself to ensure that you remain true to your identity and that the substance of the character you desire to walk in is prioritized in your daily interactions/ decisions /actions?

PART 2:

BECOMING
A CREATOR

As the mental structure comes into view and the letters and layers begin to be placed in their stations, there is a distinct feeling of anticipation. The engraved names of God and the etched declarations begin to release their demand upon creation. The blood of Jesus soaks the internal parts of the geometric structure. The whirring of the wheels begin to power up through the essences released towards the desired manifestation. As the faces of His nature begin to come into play there is a distinct sound. It is the unmistakable winds of a hurricane wrapped in water surrounded by earth and fire, forming a protective and transmutative circle around you as it carves through space and time. This encircling is not possible except through the names of God, the blood of Jesus and the laser focused will of the determined Son. The dimensions begin to open and the overwhelming wave of possibility saturates the atmosphere. As the angels gather and prepare the realms and atmospheres for both the Coming King and the direction of the one present, creation begins to turn its attention towards the one who has lifted the gate and remains in confident silence. As the union of the flames commences and turns its attention in a singular direction, the angelic host wait for the booming of its voice to determine what they should do, how they should proceed and what revelation needs to be opened so that the Manifest Son can execute the threefold will of the God in conjunction with his own.

This is the beginning of a journey that will last through the ages. It is the beginning of your own journey into the mystery of who you are in Christ and who He is in you. There is no nobler cause and there is no more difficult task. The process God has taken you through has allowed you to come this far. Now the journey begins. In your process of gaining spiritual power and coming into the realization of who you are, we ask of you one thing; remember His goodness.

SPIRITUAL INSIGHT PROMPTS

10. Insight, Intuition and Revelation
- What revelation did I gain from the meditation?
- What new understanding did I receive?
- Did I feel like what I learnt was new understanding, or a remembrance?
- What creative or inspired thoughts did I have during my meditation?
- What wisdom or understanding did I gain through my meditation?
- How did my perspective about a situation change through my meditation?
- As a result of my meditation, did I feel like I was being prompted or gently moved to shift or change something in response to the love of God? Did I gain insight of something within myself that needed to change, grow, be discarded or developed?
- Was there a something specific I identified during my meditation that I would like to take time to dig deeper into at a later stage?

11. Perception
- At any point during the meditation did I have a sensation of weightiness attached to a specific word, prayer, bible verse or thought?
- When I said the names of God, called on the blood of Jesus or engaged with the Holy Spirit, did I sense the weight of God behind my meditation?
- During my meditation did I gain an impression or perception of something outside of myself? Perhaps a sense of something in the atmosphere? Perhaps a sense of something at a global level?
- When I meditate can I perceive others in the atmosphere? Can I perceive the impact of the Church? Does it feel the same every day of the week? Do certain days in my area feel different? If there are multiple frequencies, can I separate them out and determine the strongest frequency, the weakest? Which one pulls towards me? Which one pushes away?

Sense of Movement
- During my meditation did I perceive movement? Do I sense something walking past me? Walking into the room, or out of the room? Swirling, circling, spiraling movement?
- When I meditate on things beyond myself is there an area (spiritual, global, national) that I perceive movement within?

12. Spiritual Sight
- Where is Jesus in the midst of my meditation?
- How is the Holy Spirit present in my meditation?
- Did I see any angels or beings, people from the Cloud of Witnesses, aspects of the Holy Spirit or perhaps an aspect of creation from before the fall? A

Joseph C Sturgeon II

memory contained within the flame of God?

- Did you engage any people from the Cloud of Witnesses, rabbi's, priests,
- mystics of old; dignitaries, kings or noblemen; or specific people from your own genealogy?
- Did you encounter any ancient civilizations or cities, any original cultures or ever living ones?
- During my meditation did I see any flashing light? Was there any color? Is there as specific aspect of meditation that these lights are associated with?
- Did I see a flash of any specific images held in space?
- Am I able to re-engage anything I saw at a later time?
- Is there something that I always see in meditation that I take for granted as normal?
- Did I see something unusual in meditation that I do not understand but need to describe?
- Where is the grey area or area you cannot see into? Can I focus on it and move beyond the unknown and unseeable?

13. Feelings

- Was there a predominant feeling I had during meditation? Does that feeling come from me and the things that are going on in my life? The atmosphere around me or something external (perhaps another person projecting their feelings, the Holy Spirit bringing a sense of peace and comfort?)
- During meditation was there something specific that made me feel more peaceful and relaxed? Safe?
- Did I at any stage during my meditation connect with the intense delight of God? What was it in relation to? Am I aware of the feelings of God? Delight? Exuberant joy? Compassion? Kindness?
- When I meditate on the names of God, do they elicit a specific feeling? When I encounter an angel, being or member of the Cloud of Witnesses or a specific letter of light, do I experience a specific feeling?
- When I feel something, can I turn my heart towards it and see what it is or what is causing that feeling?
- How did I feel before meditating and how did I feel after meditating? Was there a change? How long does that feeling last after meditation is finished? Does it dissipate immediately? Do I carry it throughout the day? Can I go back and access that feeling if I need refreshment and remembrance?

14. Auditory

- Can I hear sounds when I meditate? Inaudible or audible? Music or voices?
- The Psalms often talk about the sound associated with natural phenomena like the rushing waters, the galling wind, the crackling fire? Does the land I am standing on have a sound? Do I ever hear sound associated with thunder or other natural phenomena?
- Do I ever hear sound associated with movement? Crackling, whooshing?

- Is there a specific aspect of meditation or position/place I engage that is connect to a specific sound? Is that sound connected to healing? The throne? Angels singing? Is the music of the spheres present?
- Is the frequency I am hearing in one particular spot or does it pervade the atmosphere?
- Can I determine which direction the sounds are coming from? Do I only see and hear what is in front of me?
- What increases the sound? What decreases the sound? If you lean into your heart, does it increase the sound or does the sound of the waters of your heart muddy the sound you are hearing?
- Are there sounds associated with others people? Friends, family, loved ones?
- What about music connected to ancient cultures? Have I ever encountered these sounds? Or music associated with different geographical locations?

15. Olfactory and Taste

- When I meditate do I smell any fragrance at any point in my meditation? Is it sweet? Is it fruity? Is it plant like? Is it floral? Is it more ancient like old books and dusty? Is it medicinal like eucalyptus? Is it woodsy like fir or cedar? Or monastery-like, such as frankincense?
- When do the fragrances in my meditation occur? Often during moments of silent gratitude people have reported heighted sense of smell? Has that occurred for you?
- In my daily life do I ever experience or encounter a fragrance? Does that match or compliment the fragrances I encounter in my meditation?
- Do I ever experience a sweet or bitter taste during meditation?

16. Physical

- Where on my body am I feeling the presence of God? Was I acutely aware of any of my physical body parts? Perhaps my heart? My spine? My knees?
- Did I feel a sensation of heat, energy building or tingling at any point during the meditation? What was I engaging at that point in time?
- What is my preferred meditation stance? Sitting, lying standing? Is there a difference when I cross my legs and arms? Is there a difference when I meditate with my hands facing upwards? Is there a difference when I place my hand on my heart?
- Am I aware of the energy that flows through my body? During my meditation was I aware of any blockages in the flow of energy? During my meditation was I aware of my breath passing easily throughout my body?
- Can I shift the place from which I breathe? Does that change what I am able to perceive or the type of things that I am perceiving?
- Feelings sometimes are reflected as colors at the level of the body when emotion is stored in a specific body part. When I meditate do I connect feelings and colors together? Do I see specific colors residing over specific parts of my body? Can I change the colors or intensify the colors that reside at different parts of my body?

- Am I aware of places in my physical body that function as spiritual gates?
- Am I aware of these gates? Do I sense when these gates are sealed? Are they connected to God? Other people?

17. Self -Awareness and Connection

- During my meditation did I feel a strengthening of my connection to God? To the life of Christ and the hope of Christ within me? If I did communion during meditation, did I experience a sense of connection to the depth of Christ's love contained within the blood of Jesus and the voice of the blood of Jesus that speaks for us?
- Did I experience a connecting to the wisdom of God or the understanding, the mercy or the strength of God? An increased sense of confidence and inner strength resulting from my connection to Christ? (I can do all things through Christ who strengthens me)
- In my meditation did I feel an increase, build up or boost of love, life and light of God growing within me and expanding outwards? Did I feel refreshed through my meditation?
- Did my meditation increase my awareness of the unique beauty I bring to creation? A specific aspect of myself or my identity. Did it establish anything specific in my life?
- Has my meditation increased my awareness of my own voice and sound within creation?

18. Moving forward

- Different to energy heat did I maybe feel a cool air or breeze? A watery liquid movement or a fiery burning heat sensation?
- How do I honor that which I have seen, heard, smelled, tasted, felt or perceived during my meditation? Do I dismiss it as fantasy and throw it away? Do I bring it to Jesus and allow it to be held in a place of love and connection?
- What aspects of my meditation do I need to revisit? Take with me into the next meditation? It could be a specific meditation technique that elicited an insight or it could be an insight that needs to be focused on to drive it further.

GOD, THE CREATOR
INFORMING MAN
THE MAKER

Without question, God's name is a name known throughout the multiverse. At the very beginning of your Bible, you know the pages no one reads, it is called the Tetragrammaton or "Four letters." It was revealed to Moses in Exodus 3:14 and is the "strong tower" of Proverbs 18:10. When we look at the name of God there is without exaggeration millennia of revelation which has already been revealed to explore and unpack. This is in no way to say it has been completed. We do not believe it to be possible. This is to say, let us start with what has been unpacked already.

For the purposes of this journal it is important to have a basic understanding of God's name and the worlds it connects. Creation's connection to the name is what sustains it, for the name of God is our connection and revelation of all things in creation. John the Revelator said it best in Revelation 4:11 when he said, "You are worthy, our Lord and our God to receive Glory, Honor and Power. For you created all things and by your will they existed and were created."

Our ability to grasp the process of creation and becoming a creator of life is directly linked to our ability capacity to manifest the plans and purposes of God on the Earth. The structures and processes that God Himself created and embedded within creation become the prime structures we use to emulate Him and carry on the work he rested from and handed to us on the seventh day of creation. Our hope is that as you continue to explore you will expand on the very basics into the depths of what this name has to reveal and your part in continuing the work.

MEDITATION PLAN

Identity Statement

I am...

which accomplishes (associated action)

DAY	FOCUS POINT	MEDITATION PLAN
SUNDAY		
MONDAY		
TUESDAY		
WEDNESDAY		
THURSDAY		
FRIDAY		
SATURDAY		

Notes

What aspects of the nature of God are revealed within the context
of the name YHVH?

Gratitude
Today I am celebrating

Self - Awareness
Today I am noticing

Meditation
Did I follow through with my morning meditation ritual today

Y N

Spiritual Insight
During today's meditation I am sensed, saw, felt, learnt, experienced …

Manifestation

Write about the day you want to have in past tense as if it has already happened.

Sketch Space

What aspects of the nature of His creation, the pattern in which He creates and that which He emanates is revealed in the name YHVH?

Gratitude
Today I am celebrating

Self - Awareness
Today I am noticing

Meditation　　　　　　　　　　　　　　　　　　　　　　　Y　N
Did I follow through with my morning meditation ritual today

Spiritual Insight
During today's meditation I am sensed, saw, felt, learnt, experienced ...

Manifestation
Write about the day you want to have in past tense as if it has already happened.

Sketch Space

DATE & PLACE:

The Hebrew letters that comprise the alphabet are sometimes referred to as 'letters of light'. How do I experience or perceive the letters of the Name of God, as I interact with them personally?

Gratitude
Today I am celebrating

Self - Awareness
Today I am noticing

Meditation
Did I follow through with my morning meditation ritual today ☐Y ☐N

Spiritual Insight
During today's meditation I am sensed, saw, felt, learnt, experienced ...

Manifestation

Write about the day you want to have in past tense as if it has already happened.

Sketch Space

If I engage with the name Elohim or Adonai, how does that change my experience or interaction God?

Gratitude
Today I am celebrating

Self - Awareness
Today I am noticing

Meditation   Y N
Did I follow through with my morning meditation ritual today

Spiritual Insight
During today's meditation I am sensed, saw, felt, learnt, experienced ...

Manifestation

Write about the day you want to have in past tense as if it has already happened.

Sketch Space

Am I aware of any angelic movement associated with the name of God? Can I identify any specific angelic races? Specific atmospheric shifts?

Gratitude
Today I am celebrating

Self - Awareness
Today I am noticing

Meditation
Did I follow through with my morning meditation ritual today [Y] [N]

Spiritual Insight
During today's meditation I am sensed, saw, felt, learnt, experienced ...

Manifestation
Write about the day you want to have in past tense as if it has already happened.

Sketch Space

DATE & PLACE:

Consider the life of Abraham. How does the addition of the Hey (an aspect or component of the very name of God) to his name impact the course of His life? What can Abraham teach me about the name of God?

Gratitude
Today I am celebrating

Self - Awareness
Today I am noticing

Meditation Y N
Did I follow through with my morning meditation ritual today

Spiritual Insight
During today's meditation I am sensed, saw, felt, learnt, experienced ...

Manifestation

Write about the day you want to have in past tense as if it has already happened.

Sketch Space

DATE & PLACE:

From the depth of God's love, He gifted Sarah, the matriarch the addition of the lower Hey to her name such that it made her fruitful and able to bear children in her old age. What can I learn from Sarah's interaction with the name of God?

Gratitude
Today I am celebrating

Self - Awareness
Today I am noticing

Meditation
Did I follow through with my morning meditation ritual today

Y N

Spiritual Insight
During today's meditation I am sensed, saw, felt, learnt, experienced ...

Manifestation

Write about the day you want to have in past tense as if it has already happened.

Sketch Space

CREATED BY JESUS AND FOR JESUS

"For by Him all things were created that are in heaven and that are on earth, visible and invisible, whether thrones or dominions or principalities or powers. All things were created through Him and for Him." (Colossians 1:16 NKJV)

As you engage the structure of the names and grow in your capacity as a manifesting creator,, one of the most important aspects you can engage is the name of Jesus and the blood of Jesus. When Jesus is the door that you walk through, He ensures that your movement is towards God. "I am the way the truth and light, none shall pass through to the father unless through me." (John 14:6) It is His job to protect you within your movements and He is good at His job.

Engaging the cross as a transmutative device allows you to take anything to the cross and transmute it from one form to another. Ashes to beauty, mourning to the oil of gladness, despair to a garment of praise, sickness and death to life, judgement to mercy, lack to abundance. However, when you transmute anything from one form to another, when you change a situation with your declaration, when you begin to move in a particular direction with anything, there is a pendulum swing that takes place. It moves strongly in the direction that you are moving or the direction things have moved. At a certain point this pendulum swing reaches a crest and moves back towards the center with extraordinary velocity so that it can move an equal distance in the other in order to bring balance. It continues to do so until a new balance is found and it is no longer necessary to move.

People of all religions and movements around the world are aware of this natural consequence of action and give this universal law of balance various names. They have different methods of dealing with it, or softening the impact of the scales by transferring it onto their enemies. When the pendulum comes back if they are not ready it will hurt. Extreme movements have been known to cause death.

Engaging the blood of Jesus, the arc that is created by the blood that was shed before the foundations of the earth and the blood that was shed inside of time, allows one to transcends the natural laws of the universe and avert sins demand for balancing of the scales. When we engage the blood of Jesus, it covers the inside of the structure where we are and circles around us creating a barrier so when that swing comes back it does not hit us, it hits a grace-filled covenant and either moves along or comes into balance.

This is just one of the many ways Jesus protects us that we may not be aware of at all or ever. His Mercy is concurrently astounding and the greatest source of boldness and confidence available to us. I believe many will be baffled at how great His mercy continues to be in the context of our protection. As mystical as we are or think we are, there is no substitute for the blood of Jesus.

Identity Statement

I am...

which accomplishes (associated action)

DAY	FOCUS POINT	MEDITATION PLAN
SUNDAY		
MONDAY		
TUESDAY		
WEDNESDAY		
THURSDAY		
FRIDAY		
SATURDAY		

Notes

DATE & PLACE:

Jesus is the door that we move through, how aware am I of Jesus during my meditation? How can I train my consciousness to become more aware of Him as the door through which I can explore and move in the Spirit?

Gratitude
Today I am celebrating

Self - Awareness
Today I am noticing

Meditation
Did I follow through with my morning meditation ritual today

Y N

Spiritual Insight
During today's meditation I am sensed, saw, felt, learnt, experienced ...

Manifestation

Write about the day you want to have in past tense as if it has already happened.

Sketch Space

How does the arch between sacrifice that sits outside of time (the lamb slain before the foundation of the world – Rev 13:8) and the sacrifice within time (Jesus crucified on the cross), allowing man a perpetual connection point with the eternal love of God, shape my current reality?

Gratitude
Today I am celebrating

Self - Awareness
Today I am noticing

Meditation
Y N
Did I follow through with my morning meditation ritual today

Spiritual Insight
During today's meditation I am sensed, saw, felt, learnt, experienced ...

Manifestation

Write about the day you want to have in past tense as if it has already happened.

Sketch Space

Think about the five movements of the life of Christ, Christ was born, he was crucified, he died, he resurrected and rose again (or ascended). How can I align the movement of my being to the movements of Christ?

Gratitude
Today I am celebrating

Self - Awareness
Today I am noticing

Meditation
Did I follow through with my morning meditation ritual today

Y N

Spiritual Insight
During today's meditation I am sensed, saw, felt, learnt, experienced ...

Manifestation

Write about the day you want to have in past tense as if it has already happened.

Sketch Space

DATE & PLACE:

What is something that I need transmuted by the power of the cross? How does communion aid that transmutative process?

Gratitude
Today I am celebrating

Self - Awareness
Today I am noticing

Meditation   Y N
Did I follow through with my morning meditation ritual today

Spiritual Insight
During today's meditation I am sensed, saw, felt, learnt, experienced ...

Manifestation

Write about the day you want to have in past tense as if it has already happened.

Sketch Space

The blood of Jesus speaks for me, the blood of Jesus is always speaking. What is it saying? How does the voice of the blood diffuse into creation?

Gratitude
Today I am celebrating

Self - Awareness
Today I am noticing

Meditation Y N
Did I follow through with my morning meditation ritual today

Spiritual Insight
During today's meditation I am sensed, saw, felt, learnt, experienced ...

Manifestation

Write about the day you want to have in past tense as if it has already happened.

Sketch Space

What happens in my life when I engage the two-way barrier of the blood of Christ that protects me from the external? How does the blood of Christ protect me from the external repercussions that occur as a result of the shifting the scales?

Gratitude
Today I am celebrating

Self - Awareness
Today I am noticing

Meditation
Did I follow through with my morning meditation ritual today   Y N

Spiritual Insight
During today's meditation I am sensed, saw, felt, learnt, experienced ...

Manifestation

Write about the day you want to have in past tense as if it has already happened.

Sketch Space

How does the blood of Christ protect me from my internal environment; causing that which I speak, desire and pursue in purity as it is projected from me into the world? How does the blood of Jesus ensure that which I release brings forth love and life?

Gratitude
Today I am celebrating

Self - Awareness
Today I am noticing

Meditation   Y N
Did I follow through with my morning meditation ritual today

Spiritual Insight
During today's meditation I am sensed, saw, felt, learnt, experienced ...

Manifestation

Write about the day you want to have in past tense as if it has already happened.

Sketch Space

WORKING WITH THE ANGELIC HOST

How would you react if I told you I could hand you the keys that would unlock your destiny in a way you never thought was imaginable? If your answer to that statement is "it is God's job," then you still have a bit of process to go through. Everyone who has ever matured has made statements that were similar in nature. What does it mean for Jesus to be the author and perfecter of your faith? Most of my journey with God has been about searching for keys that were beyond my reach, my understanding and my ability to know. It turns out Faith works and we are still reaching. This week you will find some of the most important keys we have ever experientially discovered. The lion, the ox, the eagle and the man. The cherubs around the throne, what they represent in you and the nature of God are vital to unlock who you are in Him.

Angels are the greatest key that everyone is conceptually aware of and perpetually afraid of at the same time. My brothers and sisters in Christ love to take examples of how evil has twisted something God ordained and systematically categorize, dismiss and even warn people about it - as though God had no intention in the first place and was not the creator of such things. There has been so much fear centered about touching something unholy (using real people's life experience, trauma and mistakes) that we have both marginalized those affected and locked everyone else out of a vital part of the keys God is releasing into the Earth to unlock the doors that are shut in front of us on our respective paths to unlock our destiny. A hammer can be used to drive a nail into its place and construct a beautiful palace or to hurt someone. It is not about the hammer; it is about the intention for which it is being used. This is in no way meant to compare something as holy as an angel to a hammer but more to convey that it is the intention with which you release the angels and the station you stand in which matters.

Working with the angelic host and seeing them operate is magnificent. The ease at which they travel towards their intended goal and the resolute strength they demonstrate as they complete their task should be studied. It is without question one of the most rewarding, awe of God inspiring and at times terrifying experiences. It is not for the faint of heart or the weak-willed person who wants to casually walk-through life unaware of the realities around them. The cost is too high for many. If you want to grow in your ability, it will force you to deal with your own issues that many times you, yourself were unaware of at the time. Every time it happens it is an invitation into growth and intimacy with God. You will be stretched, you will be questioned, you will be tried and you will be tested. When you fail, as we all do, it gets harder. This in no way to deter you, it is to awaken your sense of adventure. There are dimensions and even entire realms that are waiting on you to awaken to your sonship. The direction of all of creation is in our collective hands. This is one of the keys that opens those doors.

Identity Statement

I am...

which accomplishes (associated action)

DAY	FOCUS POINT	MEDITATION PLAN
SUNDAY		
MONDAY		
TUESDAY		
WEDNESDAY		
THURSDAY		
FRIDAY		
SATURDAY		

Notes

How do I approach engaging with the angelic host?

Gratitude
Today I am celebrating

Self - Awareness
Today I am noticing

Meditation   Y N
Did I follow through with my morning meditation ritual today

Spiritual Insight
During today's meditation I am sensed, saw, felt, learnt, experienced ...

Manifestation

Write about the day you want to have in past tense as if it has already happened.

Sketch Space

What do I see, feel, experience when I engage with angels of the earth?

Gratitude
Today I am celebrating

Self - Awareness
Today I am noticing

Meditation Y N
Did I follow through with my morning meditation ritual today

Spiritual Insight
During today's meditation I am sensed, saw, felt, learnt, experienced ...

Manifestation

Write about the day you want to have in past tense as if it has already happened.

Sketch Space

What do I see, feel, experience when I engage the angels of the wind?

Gratitude
Today I am celebrating

Self - Awareness
Today I am noticing

Meditation Y N
Did I follow through with my morning meditation ritual today

Spiritual Insight
During today's meditation I am sensed, saw, felt, learnt, experienced ...

Manifestation

Write about the day you want to have in past tense as if it has already happened.

Sketch Space

What do I see feel, experience when I engage the 4 faced cherub described in Ezekiel?

Gratitude
Today I am celebrating

Self - Awareness
Today I am noticing

Meditation   Y N
Did I follow through with my morning meditation ritual today

Spiritual Insight
During today's meditation I am sensed, saw, felt, learnt, experienced …

Manifestation

Write about the day you want to have in past tense as if it has already happened.

Sketch Space

Consider the Lion and the Eagle as a combination together. What does engaging these two seemingly opposite faces produce?

Gratitude
Today I am celebrating

Self - Awareness
Today I am noticing

Meditation
Did I follow through with my morning meditation ritual today

Y N

Spiritual Insight
During today's meditation I am sensed, saw, felt, learnt, experienced ...

Manifestation

Write about the day you want to have in past tense as if it has already happened.

Sketch Space

Consider the Man and the Ox face as a combination together. What does engaging these two faces produce?

Gratitude
Today I am celebrating

Self - Awareness
Today I am noticing

Meditation
Did I follow through with my morning meditation ritual today

Y N

Spiritual Insight
During today's meditation I am sensed, saw, felt, learnt, experienced ...

Manifestation

Write about the day you want to have in past tense as if it has already happened.

Sketch Space

DATE & PLACE:

Where in my walk with God, have I encountered the cherub with the four faces? Is this only around the throne of God? Are there other places in the spirit where this angelic being is experienced?

Gratitude
Today I am celebrating

Self - Awareness
Today I am noticing

Meditation   Y N
Did I follow through with my morning meditation ritual today

Spiritual Insight
During today's meditation I am sensed, saw, felt, learnt, experienced ...

Manifestation

Write about the day you want to have in past tense as if it has already happened.

Sketch Space

SUBSTANCE OF CREATION

Everything in manifested creation is created from one or more of the 4 elements. Consider your physical body, it was created from dust (Genesis), it contains water, the heat or fire from the blood and the breath that you breathe is considered the wind.

Fire is the transmutative substance of the cosmos. It is the ascender's friend and the purifier of hearts. It is the one of the substances that molds and shapes situations and circumstances. It changes the landscape in both the natural as well as in the spirit. It beckons holiness and, wielded correctly, it can destroy darkness and wreak havoc in the enemy's camp. It is the language used to describe essential aspects of your relationship with God while perfectly describing His protection and His Love. The flame roars and expands as your will is exerted and calms as the next move is positioned. It is the language used to describe the beginning and the end. Fire is your best friend and your worst enemy. It is to be handled with care.

Earth is the vessel. It is the containment center that holds all the other elements. Moses struck the rock and water came out. Your body is the Earthen vessel that holds your blood (fire), your water (body is over 70%) and wind (your breath). Without earth there is no crucible for the reaction God wants to produce to be created and housed. Earth is the ground that is plowed by the ox, soared over by the eagle, carved and provided for by the water and scorched by the fire. It is the centerpiece of the multiverse and the house of the access for all of creation back to God.

Wind is the harmonizer. It creates beauty out of chaos and brings balance into mercy. Wind is the torrent that rips up while also being the cool breeze that blows against your face. It can be fiercely violent or refreshingly calm. It can be the approaching of a storm or a sign that God is with you. Without wind, we would not know relief from a scorching sun or a fresh new beginning to the day. Wind is power and wind is a gift.

Water ebbs and flows like the oceans' tide. It is the sustenance of one's being and becomes the substance without which man cannot survive in the desert. The river of life that feeds the trees that reside on its banks. Waters also allude to provision and prosperity, yet it also water that is used to describe the liquidity of the waters of the soul, the fluidity of the movement of the lower heavens and the refreshment of the mercy of God. Its reflective quality is seen in the stillness of the sea of glass allowing one to look into the waters and gaze upon the reflection. These same waters can depict a chaos and turbulence. The place of sea monsters and chaos where only the brave dare to reach into, to draw forth life. The pounding of the waves against the rocks, as deep cries out to deep in the roar of the waterfalls. It is the waters that are used for baptism, the waters that open dimensions, the parting of the waters that allow the Israelites to cross into the desert, the breaking of the waters that signals the birth of a child. It is the emersion of Jesus from the waters after His baptism that caused the descension of the Holy Spirit and the Water allows that which is above to descend and become manifest.

Identity Statement

I am...

_____

_____

which accomplishes (associated action)

_____

_____

_____

DAY	FOCUS POINT	MEDITATION PLAN
SUNDAY		
MONDAY		
TUESDAY		
WEDNESDAY		
THURSDAY		
FRIDAY		
SATURDAY		

Notes

_____

_____

Am I aware of the substance that God used to mold and create me, to knit me together? Am I aware of the waters within, the fire (blood) within, the breath within? How does this connect with the waters above, blood of Jesus and the breath of the Holy Spirit?

Gratitude
Today I am celebrating

Self - Awareness
Today I am noticing

Meditation
Y N

Did I follow through with my morning meditation ritual today

Spiritual Insight
During today's meditation I am sensed, saw, felt, learnt, experienced ...

Manifestation

Write about the day you want to have in past tense as if it has already happened.

Sketch Space

Am I aware of the elements that comprise of heaven? Have I noticed in the Bible places where descriptions of God, His throne, His voice are correlated with natural weather phenomena? Why does the Bible use these descriptions?

Gratitude
Today I am celebrating

Self - Awareness
Today I am noticing

Meditation
Did I follow through with my morning meditation ritual today Y N

Spiritual Insight
During today's meditation I am sensed, saw, felt, learnt, experienced ...

Manifestation

Write about the day you want to have in past tense as if it has already happened.

Sketch Space

DATE & PLACE:

Think about all the possible type of water from the gentle stream, to the violent waves of a stormy sea crashing against the rocks, the refreshment of the river, the stillness of the morning lake to the vastness and depth of the ocean, the waterfall, the rain and even the way the moon governs the tides and its connection to water. Consider all the angelic that contain part water as their make up; the water of the soul; the sea of glass and the river beneath the throne in the Book of Revelation. Spend some time contemplating water connected to the Creator who created it, in connection to Yahweh.

Gratitude
Today I am celebrating

Self - Awareness
Today I am noticing

Meditation   Y N
Did I follow through with my morning meditation ritual today

Spiritual Insight
During today's meditation I am sensed, saw, felt, learnt, experienced ...

Manifestation

Write about the day you want to have in past tense as if it has already happened.

Sketch Space

DATE & PLACE:

Think about all the possible type of fire, heat and flames from the burning bush, the blue flame of the Yechida, the mysterious flame that was in the temple; the burning hot and burning cold fire; the ministers that are like flames of fire; the seraphim and all other fiery beings; think about fiery emotions, even tongues of fire during Pentecost and spend some time contemplating fire in connection with the name Elohim.

Gratitude
Today I am celebrating

Self - Awareness
Today I am noticing

Meditation   Y N
Did I follow through with my morning meditation ritual today

Spiritual Insight
During today's meditation I am sensed, saw, felt, learnt, experienced ...

Manifestation

Write about the day you want to have in past tense as if it has already happened.

Sketch Space

Think about all the possible types of earth, the cosmic dust from which Adam was formed, the soil in which the seed is planted; the earth that produces life and crops; the mountains that form the high places; the rocks and the metals, gemstones, the foundation stone, the cornerstone, the house that is built upon the rock and molding the clay. Spend some time contemplating earth and its connection to the living God, the Creator.

Gratitude
Today I am celebrating

Self - Awareness
Today I am noticing

Meditation   Y N
Did I follow through with my morning meditation ritual today

Spiritual Insight
During today's meditation I am sensed, saw, felt, learnt, experienced ...

Manifestation

Write about the day you want to have in past tense as if it has already happened.

Sketch Space

DATE & PLACE:

Think about all the possible types of wind; harmonizing wind, gentle breeze, tornado, breath in your lungs, the very first breath a child breathes, breath in the atmosphere, noble inert gases, the wind that no one knows where it comes from and where it is going, the wind the brings forth rain, the warm summer or mountain wind, a cool ocean breeze or even the breath of life that God breathed upon Adam. Spend some time contemplating the wind and its connection to Ruach Hakodesh.

Gratitude
Today I am celebrating

Self - Awareness
Today I am noticing

Meditation   Y N
Did I follow through with my morning meditation ritual today

Spiritual Insight
During today's meditation I am sensed, saw, felt, learnt, experienced ...

Manifestation

Write about the day you want to have in past tense as if it has already happened.

Sketch Space

Moses in the Old Testament had many interactions and miracles that occurred as elemental miracles. From parting the waters, to turning the bitter waters sweet and even even hitting the rock and bringing forth water. He had miracles of fire including the burning bush, there were miracles of manna coming down from heaven. What was Moses' interaction with water and fire? What does the interaction of water and fire produce?

Gratitude
Today I am celebrating

Self - Awareness
Today I am noticing

Meditation   Y N
Did I follow through with my morning meditation ritual today

Spiritual Insight
During today's meditation I am sensed, saw, felt, learnt, experienced ...

Manifestation

Write about the day you want to have in past tense as if it has already happened.

Sketch Space

ADDITIONAL PROMPTS

The structure as a whole:

- How can I use the structures we have learned to not only grow but to activate the favor of God?
- How do I experience, see, visualize being encircled by the Names of God?
- What does the experience of continuous connection to the throne room
- frequency and carrying the frequency of the very Name of God around my entire being mean to me? How does it empower my daily life?
- How do my "I am" declarations interact with the Name of God at every level?
- How does my determined set will interact with the frequency of the Name of God?

Week 1: The four-letter name of God

- How does four letter name of God interact with the four chambers of my heart?
- How do you feel when you are stressed and breath the name of God? What does your breath, connected to the Name do?
- When I think of Yod as the seed, and I know the seed is planted in the blood. How does this deepen my understanding of the seed that grows into the Tree of Life? How does it impact my understand of faith as a mustard seed? Are all seeds the same?
- Can I conceptualize the upper and lower Hebrew letter Hey as gateways to be ascended through into the mystery of the Godhead? What about the two Heh's as gateways within the name of God to descend and bring things into manifestation?
- How does my interaction with Vav, as a nail or a connection between two worlds, impact my understanding of the nails that were place in the hands of Jesus as he hung on the cross? What then does the cross of Christ symbolize?

Week 2: The name of Jesus

- When I engage the name of Jesus, what angelic respond?
- When I engage the blood of Jesus, what moves towards me and away from me? (Be more specific than 'angels' and 'demons').
- When I soak something in the blood of Jesus, what is the result?
- When I want to create a protective barrier around something, how does the blood of Jesus form that?
- What is my level of awareness of experiencing Jesus as my access to the spirit realm? How aware am I of the blood of Jesus that forms a barrier between creation and eternity? What does my interaction with that blood look or feel like?
- Am I aware that I can call out and instantly see Jesus no matter where I am in the Spirit? Have I ever done this? In what situations is this important for me to practice?
- How aware am I of not only the presence of Jesus but His emotions, His

thoughts, His guidance, His love when I am moving in the spirit?

- How does adding the Shin interact with the name YHVH? With the name Jesus?
- What does the life of Christ and the glory of the Son in its diffusion through creation feel like when I am positioned outside of creation?
- What is the importance of the cross, the Hebrew letter Tav, and its significance as a place of exchange, an ability to transmute for us as Christians?

Week 3: The 4 faced cherub

- We know the King Jesus Lion, the ferocious one that attacks every enemy. What happens when you engage Him?
- What type of ground does the Ox stay away from?
- When the eagle is soaring, what are its eyes looking at?
- What can the man become? What are the man's different forms?
- Is there a connection between the star constellations that God created: Leo, Taurus (Ox), Aquarius (man) and the four faces described in Ezekiel?
- What is the connection between the Lion of Judah, the tribe of Judah that goes first, the role of Kingship and the Lion face?
- When you engage the Man face, what is the image of man that you see? Is it Adam? Is it man that exists in creation now? Adam that existed before the fall?

Week 4: Molding the substances of creation

- How does the Fire, Earth, Wind and Water react when you engage the name of Jesus at this point? Does it react differently when you engage the name of Jesus in an ascended place?
- When you extend your hand towards the Earth what happens in the space between your hand and the Earth?
- How do I harmonize the various elements through my connection to Christ?
- Why is it so important that I always connect the elements to the name of God and do not engage them outside of this name?
- Why were most ancient practices of medicine a discussion around elemental balance? How does my body relate to the elements and how can I balance the elements within my body using the Name of God?
- Consider the miracles performed in the New Testament. Jesus spat on the ground (earth and water) and healed the blind man (John 9:6). How does manipulation of the elements play a role in the many of the healing miracles that occur in the New Testament? Why is this important? What does this mean for believers? How does this impact our understanding of signs, wonders and miracles?
- Is manipulation of elements a function of the spirit or the soul? Consider movies like 'The Matrix' where the spoon is bent. What aspect of your being is involved in manipulating elements?
- How does the Holy Spirit interact with the elements? What is her role considering things like tongues of fire? Being compared to the wind? Breath over the water?

CREATING RITUALS TO INCREASE INTENTIONALITY

The word ritual often has a bad reputation. For the onlooker it can often conjure up an image of legalistic rules and a series of actions done by the partaker in a specific sequence to elicit some sort of outcome. It is often assumed that a ritual robs the partaker of a depth of experience or even the vaguest sense of affection. However, this description is not a ritual but rather a routine devoid of intent, awareness and conjured from a sense of duty devoid of love. A demonstration without the involvement of one's heart. Another negative connotation of rituals is its association with deep magic and the occult, the rituals of witchcraft, or the rituals of etc. However, I want to encourage you today to re-look and reconsider the concept of rituals (rather than running away from a word that has been inaccurately used to describe things that exist outside of the tender love of God).

Rituals are actually beautiful traditions, often ceremonies or feasts, that encompass the beauty of experiential access to God that moves beyond routine. For the onlooker it might seem rigid and entrenched in discipline rather than spontaneity. However, for the partaker who intentionally engages the activity with the fullness of their heart affection, the unwavering focus of their minds attention the ritual can provide a powerful life altering experience and encounter with divinity.

Rituals don't have to be complicated. Consider the rituals that we perform in our daily lives such as saying grace before a meal. This action, without setting the intention of the heart or focusing one's gaze, can be merely a tradition void of meaning. However, it can also be a way of both tuning oneself to the presence of God and creating a gate for everyone participating in the meal to experience and partake in Christ's abundant life prior to eating the food. Perhaps the ritual is your morning meditation. You can chant the name of God without involving your heart. To some extent there will be a change on a cellular level as a result of quantum entanglement but when the heart intent is fixed, the gaze is set towards the Name of God, a gate into obtaining a deeper experience of God becomes available. The intent of the heart is pivotal for creating meaning to a ritual opposed to a routine that is done out of obligation and discipline or duty.

Furthermore, when one participates in rituals that go beyond our current moment, we connect with both the past, present and future. When we partake in communion, not only are we connecting with the blood of Christ before the foundation of the world, we are joining and cojoining ourselves and our essence with every Christian that makes up the body of Christ both in our present time, in generations that have past and generations that are still to come. When we say the set prayers of our forefathers, or engage in creating mental edifies that comprise of some of the mysteries that have practiced in secret over many generations, we position ourselves to stand amongst those that have gone before us at a level otherwise unattainable.

Rituals connected to the ancients. The practices of those that have gone before protect us from our obsession with individuality driven by our ego, and reunite us with the concept of the body of Christ both as a believer inside of time and the body that exists outside of time. Rituals that are not related to self-care but the Kingdom help us move to a macro-perspective of global activity and create an intrinsic awareness of global spiritual movements. Finally, rituals connected to the blood of Christ, connect us to that 'everything' in creation, both inside and outside of time. "For by Him all things were created that are in heaven and that are on earth, visible and invisible, whether thrones or dominions or principalities or powers. All things were created through Him and for Him," (Colossians 1:16). Spiritual Rituals, for the intentional partaker leave a mark of awe and a deepened affection for our God.

For the purpose of this journal, we want to encourage you to create your own intentional ritual. It could be a self-care type activity that allows you to feel more refreshed and have more time with God. Activities such as the art sitting in silence for 5 minutes every morning, practicing gratitude, drinking a coffee or even just appreciating some form of natural beauty each day which could include a sunset, mountain path or simply a beautiful flower. However, the ritual could also embrace some of our spiritual traditions passed down the generations from the Bible. This could include communion, or the creeds that establish the tenants of our faith or even saying grace at a meal. It could include some of the spiritual structures we have learnt to create, or some of the engagements we do with the name of God. No matter the activity or ritual you chose to pursue, the main purpose of this exercise is to consciously think and write down the affection and gaze of the heart during this ritual, the attention and focus of the mind and to increase conscious awareness of your internal stature and stance during these practices.

Ritual 1:

The activity

Where is my heart's affection set during this ritual? What is the focus of my mind during this ritual? What is my intention for this ritual?

Ritual 2:

The activity

_____

_____

_____

_____

_____

_____

_____

_____

Where is my heart's affection set during this ritual? What is the focus of my mind during this ritual? What is my intention for this ritual?

_____

_____

_____

_____

_____

_____

_____

_____

_____

_____

_____

_____

_____

_____

_____

Ritual 3:

The activity

_____

_____

_____

_____

_____

_____

_____

_____

Where is my heart's affection set during this ritual? What is the focus of my mind during this ritual? What is my intention for this ritual?

_____

_____

_____

_____

_____

_____

_____

_____

_____

_____

_____

_____

_____

Now that you have spent some time thinking about your affection, attention, focus and desired intent for these rituals, start practicing them and see if this activity increases your awareness and experiential encounter. Try do one ritual every-day for the month ahead.

PART 3:

HARMONIZING THE GLOBAL INFLOW

The beauty of a world completely in harmony with its Creator has been dreamed about since before its foundation. Man, in the fullness of his destiny was the before- proclaimed harmonizer. It was humankind who was to make Earth look like Heaven and it was the self-same who was given the seat of authority, not only over the Earth, but of all creation. Earth is just the beginning and we are epochs away from accomplishing the first call.

The inflow of what and who moves in and out of the Earth is also our responsibility. We are designed to be the keepers of justice and mercy and the purveyors of beauty to the cosmos. It begins not with the whole world but with our own lives. We are perpetually engaged in the microcosm of the macrocosm. If we can be trusted with little, we will be given much. This is our promise, this is our desire, this is our destiny - to not only harmonize the globe but to express the beauty of divinity to all of creation.

SPIRITUAL INSIGHT PROMPTS

19. Insight, Intuition and Revelation

- What revelation did I gain from the meditation?
- What new understanding did I receive?
- Did I feel like what I learnt was new understanding, or a remembrance?
- What creative or inspired thoughts did I have during my meditation?
- What wisdom or understanding did I gain through my meditation?
- How did my perspective about a situation change through my meditation?
- As a result of my meditation, did I feel like I was being prompted or gently moved to shift or change something in response to the love of God? Did I gain insight of something within myself that needed to change, grow, be discarded or developed?
- Was there a something specific I identified during my meditation that I would like to take time to dig deeper into at a later stage?

20. Perception

- At any point during the meditation did I have a sensation of weightiness attached to a specific word, prayer, bible verse or thought?
- When I said the names of God, called on the blood of Jesus or engaged with the Holy Spirit did I sense the weight of God behind my meditation?
- During my meditation did I gain an impression or perception of something outside of myself? Perhaps a sense of something in the atmosphere? Perhaps a sense of something at a global level?
- When I meditate can I perceive others in the atmosphere? Can I perceive the impact of the Church? Does it feel the same every day of the week? Do certain days in my area feel different? If there are multiple frequencies, can I separate them out and determine the strongest frequency, the weakest? Which one pulls towards me? Which one pushes away?

Sense of Movement

- During my meditation did I perceive movement? Do I sense something walking past me? Walking into the room, or out of the room? Swirling, circling, spiraling movement?
- When I meditate on things beyond myself is there an area (spiritual, global, national) that I perceive movement within?

21. Spiritual Sight

- Where is Jesus in the midst of my meditation?
- How is the Holy Spirit present in my meditation?
- Did I see any angels or beings, people from the Cloud of Witnesses, aspects of the Holy Spirit or perhaps an aspect of creation from before the fall? A memory contained within the flame of God?

- Did you engage any people from the Cloud of Witnesses, rabbi's, priests, mystics of old; dignitaries, kings or noblemen; or specific people from your own genealogy?
- Did you encounter any ancient civilizations or cities, any original cultures or ever
- living ones?
- During my meditation did I see any flashing light? Was there any color? Is there
- as specific aspect of meditation that these lights are associated with?
- Did I see a flash of any specific images held in space?
- Am I able to re-engage anything I saw at a later time?
- Is there something that I always see in meditation that I take for granted as normal?
- Did I see something unusual in meditation that I do not understand but need to describe?
- Where is the grey area or area you cannot see into? Can I focus on it and move beyond the unknown and unseeable?

22. Feelings

- Was there a predominant feeling I had during meditation? Does that feeling come from me and the things that are going on in my life? The atmosphere around me or something external (perhaps another person projecting their feelings, the Holy Spirit bringing a sense of peace and comfort?)
- During meditation was there something specific that made me feel more peaceful and relaxed? Safe?
- Did I at any stage during my meditation with the intense delight of God? What was it in relation to? Am I aware of the feelings of God? Delight? Exuberant joy? Compassion? Kindness?
- When I meditate on the names of God, do they elicit a specific feeling? When I encounter an angel, being or member of the Cloud of Witnesses or a specific letter of light do I experience a specific feeling?
- When I feel something can I turn my heart towards it and see what it is or what is causing that feeling?
- How did I feel before meditating and how did I feel after meditating? Was there a change? How long does that feeling last after meditation is finished? Does it dissipate immediately? Do I carry throughout the day? Can I go back and access that feeling if I need refreshment and remembrance?

23. Auditory

- Can I hear sounds when I meditate? Inaudible or audible? Music or voices?
- The Psalms often talk about the sound associated with natural phenomena like the rushing waters, the galling wind, the crackling fire? Does the land I am standing on have a sound? Do I ever hear sound associated with thunder or other natural phenomena?
- Do I ever hear sound associated with movement? Crackling, whooshing?
- Is there a specific aspect of meditation or position/place I engage that is connect to a specific sound? Is that sound connected to healing? The throne?

Angels singing? Is the music of the spheres present?

- Is the frequency I am hearing in one particular spot or does it pervade the atmosphere?
- Can I determine which direction the sounds are coming from? Do I only see and hear what is in front of me?
- What increases the sound? What decreases the sound? If you lean into your heart, does it increase the sound or does the sound of the waters of your heart muddy the sound you are hearing?
- Are there sounds associated with others people? Friends, family, loved ones?
- What about music connected to ancient cultures? Have I ever encountered these sounds? Or music associated with different geographical locations?

24. Olfactory and Taste

- When I meditate do I smell any fragrance at any point in my meditation? Is it sweet? Is it fruity? Is it plant like? Is it floral? Is it more ancient like old books and dusty? Is it medicinal like eucalyptus? Is it woodsy like fir or cedar? Or monastery-like, such as frankincense?
- When do the fragrances in my meditation occur? Often during moments of silent gratitude people have reported heighted sense of smell? Has that occurred for you?
- In my daily life do I ever experience or encounter a fragrance? Does that match or compliment the fragrances I encounter in my meditation?
- Do I ever experience a sweet or bitter taste during meditation?

25. Physical

- Where on my body am I feeling the presence of God? Was I acutely aware of any of my physical body parts? Perhaps my heart? My spine? My knees?
- Did I feel a sensation of heat, energy building or tingling at any point during the meditation? What was I engaging at that point in time?
- What is my preferred meditation stance? Sitting, lying standing? Is there a difference when I cross my legs and arms? Is there a difference when I meditate with my hands facing upwards? Is there a difference when I place my hand on my heart?
- Am I aware of the energy that flows through my body? During my meditation was I aware of any blockages in the flow of energy? During my meditation was I aware of my breath passing easily throughout my body?
- Can I shift the place from which I breathe? Does that change what I am able to perceive or the type of things that I am perceiving?
- Feelings sometimes are reflected as colors at the level of the body when emotion is stored in a specific body part. When I meditate do I connect feelings and colors together? Do I see specific colors residing over specific parts of my body? Can I change the colors or intensify the colors that reside at different parts of my body?
- Am I aware of places in my physical body that function as spiritual gates? Am I aware of these gates? Do I sense when these gates are sealed? Are they connected to God? Other people?

26. Self-Awareness and Connection

- During my meditation did I feel a strengthening of my connection to God? To the life of Christ and the hope of Christ within me? If I did communion during meditation, did I experience a sense of connection to the depth of Christ's love contained within the blood of Jesus and the voice of the blood of Jesus that speaks for us?

- Did I experience a connecting to the wisdom of God or the understanding, the mercy or the strength of God? An increased sense of confidence and inner strength resulting from my connection to Christ? (I can do all things through Christ who strengthens me)

- In my meditation did I feel an increase, build up or boost of love, life and light of God growing within me and expanding outwards? Did I feel refreshed through my meditation?

- Did my meditation increase my awareness of the unique beauty I bring to creation? A specific aspect of myself or my identity. Did it establish anything specific in my life?

- Has my meditation increased my awareness of my own voice and sound within creation?

27. Moving forward

- Different to energy heat did I maybe feel a cool air or breeze? A watery liquid movement or a fiery burning heat sensation?

- How do I honor that which I have seen, heard, smelled, tasted, felt or perceived during my meditation? Do I dismiss it as fantasy and throw it away? Do I bring it to Jesus and allow it to be held in a place of love and connection?

- What aspects of my meditation do I need to revisit? Take with me into the next meditation? It could be a specific meditation technique that elicited an insight or it could be an insight that needs to be focused on to drive it further.

JUDGEMENT AND MERCY

For the righteous of God there is an art in the ability to harmonize Judgement and Mercy that moves away from a bipartisan scale designed to promote fairness through equal parts, karma and any other system where the snake that bites its own tail is upheld (like the system of Libra that weighs and judges everything on a scale and finds man wanting). "You have been weighed on the scales and found wanting," (Daniel 5:27). Yet for the man or woman of God who is made righteous not by his own righteousness but rather by Christ Jesus who had no sin, they are lifted above the scale of natural laws, above the measuring system of man's deficiency and the universe's demand for payment.

For the believer, the blood of Christ is placed on either side of the scale, rendering the scale void of its ability to measure deficit or sin. We see this in Proverbs 16:11; "weights and scales are the Lord's." This is further reiterated by the verse 1 Peter 4:17; "For the Judgements begins at the house of God." Yet even though there is no condemnation for those in Christ (Romans 8:1), it seems that many of us keep tuning our inner being towards judgment both of self and others, placing various aspects of our lives back onto the scales of judgment, despite being set free and free indeed by Christ (John 8:32 paraphrased). The mercy of God endures forever.

It is the mature believer who is able to tilt the global scales directing the streams of mercy that enter the earth towards humanity causing it to rain on both the just and the unjust (Matt 5:45). It is the powerful man or women of God that, instead of condemning those that are not a part of their specific tribe and joining the cycle of the oppressed, becoming the oppressor, choses to dig deep into the well of their foundation and pulls up vessels of mercy such that the refreshment of the morning dew and the streams of compassion can be experienced by all those that sit beneath their shadow.

There are two types of judgement that should be mentioned here. 'Soft judgement' which is correction, and 'Harsh judgement'. Surprisingly both of them are acts of Mercy. Correction is to help you along the path. For the purposes of explaining harsh judgement let us briefly look at Noah. The whole world was judged but it was for the preservation of the seed of humanity. As hard as it is for most people to understand or comprehend, sometimes a King kills his enemies to protect his own family. It is an act of harsh judgement towards others but an act of mercy towards his own family. This is the case with Noah and many others in the Bible.

Kings use judgement as a tool to produce mercy for their kingdom by drawing things into the correct alignment rather than condemning nations to death. Jesus took judgement upon Himself so that mercy could be displayed to all creation.

Identity Statement

I am...

_____

_____

which accomplishes (associated action)

_____

_____

DAY	FOCUS POINT	MEDITATION PLAN
SUNDAY		
MONDAY		
TUESDAY		
WEDNESDAY		
THURSDAY		
FRIDAY		
SATURDAY		

Notes

_____

_____

Judgement against self: What areas in my life am I self-judgmental? Are there things that I try to put back onto the scales of judgement rather than allowing the grace and mercy of God to render the scales void of its ability to measure me.

Gratitude
Today I am celebrating

Self - Awareness
Today I am noticing

Meditation
Did I follow through with my morning meditation ritual today

Y N

Spiritual Insight
During today's meditation I am sensed, saw, felt, learnt, experienced ...

Manifestation

Write about the day you want to have in past tense as if it has already happened.

Sketch Space

Judgement against others: who or what do I judge and demand payment both literal and figurative? Is there a double standard for what I expect of others compared to what God says? How does my personal bias and connection to my own tribe drive my judgement of others?

Gratitude
Today I am celebrating

Self - Awareness
Today I am noticing

Meditation   Y N
Did I follow through with my morning meditation ritual today

Spiritual Insight
During today's meditation I am sensed, saw, felt, learnt, experienced ...

Manifestation

Write about the day you want to have in past tense as if it has already happened.

Sketch Space

How do I retrain my reactive instinct to assume a stance of mercy rather than move to the defensive position of judgement?

Gratitude
Today I am celebrating

Self - Awareness
Today I am noticing

Meditation
Did I follow through with my morning meditation ritual today

Y N

Spiritual Insight
During today's meditation I am sensed, saw, felt, learnt, experienced ...

Manifestation

Write about the day you want to have in past tense as if it has already happened.

Sketch Space

On a global level, judgement is defined as bringing things into correct alignment. How do I participate in bringing things into alignment with God's will and God's mercy? How do I emit righteous judgement from the position of being a King? What does that tangibly look like?

Gratitude
Today I am celebrating

Self - Awareness
Today I am noticing

Meditation
Did I follow through with my morning meditation ritual today   [Y] [N]

Spiritual Insight
During today's meditation I am sensed, saw, felt, learnt, experienced ...

Manifestation

Write about the day you want to have in past tense as if it has already happened.

Sketch Space

It is said that building a vessel of mercy, so that all judgement moves from a place of mercy, is crucial for righteous governance to occur. What does building a vessel of mercy entail? How can I daily build vessels of Mercy?

Gratitude
Today I am celebrating

Self - Awareness
Today I am noticing

Meditation   ☐Y ☐N
Did I follow through with my morning meditation ritual today

Spiritual Insight
During today's meditation I am sensed, saw, felt, learnt, experienced ...

Manifestation

Write about the day you want to have in past tense as if it has already happened.

Sketch Space

DATE & PLACE:

His mercy is made new every morning (Lamentation 3:22-23). Mercy is like the morning cloud/dew (Hosea 6:4). Contemplate the connection between the morning dew and the refreshment that comes from the mercy of God. How can we break the stored-up vessels of mercy over those in our lives who need refreshment?

Gratitude
Today I am celebrating

Self - Awareness
Today I am noticing

Meditation
Did I follow through with my morning meditation ritual today   Y N

Spiritual Insight
During today's meditation I am sensed, saw, felt, learnt, experienced ...

Manifestation

Write about the day you want to have in past tense as if it has already happened.

Sketch Space

DATE & PLACE:

God caused it to rain on the righteous and unrighteous. How do we tangibly stay the arm of judgement and direct the refreshing streams of mercy towards humanity?

Gratitude
Today I am celebrating

Self - Awareness
Today I am noticing

Meditation
Did I follow through with my morning meditation ritual today

Y N

Spiritual Insight
During today's meditation I am sensed, saw, felt, learnt, experienced ...

Manifestation
Write about the day you want to have in past tense as if it has already happened.

Sketch Space

DEATH AND LIFE

This week we are considering the harmonizing of death and life and how the cross transmuted death to life by the process of resurrection. Turning that which was meant to die in a state of finality and remain dead into life bursting forth into abundance. Life that can never die - eternal life.

There are multiple themes that exist within this form of transmutation and harmonization. The first is the concept of death and sacrifice. There is both a destructive death, and a dying to oneself daily. The destructive death entering the world as a consequence of the fall and needs to be transmuted by the blood of Christ. If left unchanged the power of judgement becomes deconstructive and continues to allow the resonance of death to enter our cells, organs and body. However, if we learn to transmute the power of judgement into glory rather than death by the blood of our Lord Jesus Christ, the light contained within the blood is transmitted into our cells, organs and body, producing the abundance of life, healing all diseases (in the case of Christ transfiguration of His physical body). Communion is vital for the intertwining of Christ's blood and Christ's love and the tangible power of the cross into our physical daily lives.

The second place we encounter this concept of "death" is one that is more a fear rather than a finality. It occurs when we encounter the holiness of God, as He takes His seat upon the throne surrounded by myriads and myriads of angels each crying out, "Holy, Holy, Holy". This sight can cause even the bravest of men to tremble under the weight and saturation of His presence. Holiness for some can feel like death but it is from His holiness that glory is exuded and signs, miracles, healing and abundant life begins to flow through the veins of those whose faces radiate this reflected light.

And finally, in this place of transmuting death to life, there is the role of the priest and the concept of sacrifice. The Christian who is sanctified by Christ is called a royal and holy priesthood and there is a sacrificial handing over and releasing of that which the soul clings too. A surrendering to God as such. Some would call this concept "dying to self" but we believe and have seen much more fruit in focusing on the process of surrender and handing over issues to God in order that we can focus on more of Him. Too many have spent so much time focusing on what is wrong that they have completely lost their ability to see beauty. A re-training of focus is needed as well as a completely new understanding of the nature of our soul. In this process of the "putting off of the old" and "putting on the new," the best possible way is as we focus and learn more of the depths of God. As issues inevitably come up, we learn from Him more about ourselves and are changed in our thinking and our understanding. In this place of awe, releasing the death our soul still clings to and transmuting our understanding from a place of death to life, our capacity to not only see beauty but to transform everything around us into this place is born again.

It is only from a place of death and dying that Christ rose and was resurrected.

Identity Statement

I am...

which accomplishes (associated action)

DAY	FOCUS POINT	MEDITATION PLAN
SUNDAY		
MONDAY		
TUESDAY		
WEDNESDAY		
THURSDAY		
FRIDAY		
SATURDAY		

Notes

There are some things in life that need to die in order for the space of new opportunities, new creativity and even new relationships to occur. What are some of the things that need to be brought to an end in my life? What are some things that I am carrying or holding onto that are past their due date? These could be literal or figurative such as friendship, project, relationship or even a pattern of behavior.

Gratitude
Today I am celebrating

Self - Awareness
Today I am noticing

Meditation
Did I follow through with my morning meditation ritual today
Y N

Spiritual Insight
During today's meditation I am sensed, saw, felt, learnt, experienced ...

Manifestation

Write about the day you want to have in past tense as if it has already happened.

Sketch Space

DATE & PLACE:

Consider the verse, "Unless a seed falls to the ground and dies it will only bear single fruit but if it dies it bear much fruit," (John 12:24). Sometimes a seed needs to die and be placed in the blood of Christ so that it can be infused with the abundant life of Christ and multiply. Our attachment to the seed can be what limits its impact. Choosing to place it on the cross/ altar, removing our attachment, drenching it in the blood and entrusting God to nurture, grow and harvest it can have far reaching affects. What seeds in my life do I need to place on the altar and drench in the blood of Christ?

Gratitude
Today I am celebrating

Self - Awareness
Today I am noticing

Meditation   Y N
Did I follow through with my morning meditation ritual today

Spiritual Insight
During today's meditation I am sensed, saw, felt, learnt, experienced ...

Manifestation

Write about the day you want to have in past tense as if it has already happened.

Sketch Space

Drenching things in the blood of Christ is not only for things that need to be surrendered, but also things that have been worked at and stored up over time. This could be building of soul essence placed within the blood of Christ. It could be excellence in your professional arena, it could be hard work, virtue or something that required discipline like growing patience and love. All of these seeds when placed within the blood are given the capacity to multiply and be harvested at a later time in your life.

Gratitude
Today I am celebrating

Self - Awareness
Today I am noticing

Meditation
Did I follow through with my morning meditation ritual today

Y N

Spiritual Insight
During today's meditation I am sensed, saw, felt, learnt, experienced ...

Manifestation

Write about the day you want to have in past tense as if it has already happened.

Sketch Space

If something does not die it can not be resurrected? What are the dreams and desires, the seeds in my life that I have allowed to die that now need to be resurrected or harvested?

Gratitude
Today I am celebrating

Self - Awareness
Today I am noticing

Meditation   Y N
Did I follow through with my morning meditation ritual today

Spiritual Insight
During today's meditation I am sensed, saw, felt, learnt, experienced ...

Manifestation

Write about the day you want to have in past tense as if it has already happened.

Sketch Space

The ability to resurrect is deeply connected to Christ's abundant life, vitality, vibrancy. How do I daily celebrate the vitality, brilliance, vibrancy of explosive abundant life to the full that has been given to me through Christ?

Gratitude
Today I am celebrating

Self - Awareness
Today I am noticing

Meditation
Did I follow through with my morning meditation ritual today   Y N

Spiritual Insight
During today's meditation I am sensed, saw, felt, learnt, experienced ...

Manifestation

Write about the day you want to have in past tense as if it has already happened.

Sketch Space

Many people in the world have had visions of themselves as 200 and 300 years old, still alive. Immortality has become a huge point of interest to many (especially those over fifty!). Is this physical body the only one I have? Is physicality only for this world or is it in the ages to come as well? How many bodies do I have and how do I begin to connect with all of them? (See 1 Corinthians 15 for reference).

Gratitude
Today I am celebrating

Self - Awareness
Today I am noticing

Meditation
Did I follow through with my morning meditation ritual today

Y N

Spiritual Insight
During today's meditation I am sensed, saw, felt, learnt, experienced ...

Manifestation
Write about the day you want to have in past tense as if it has already happened.

Sketch Space

DATE & PLACE:

One of the biggest hindrances to ascension is the fear of death. Your physical body does not know for sure if you leave that you will come back. Believing the opposite of a fear does not nullify or deal with that fear. The best way to deal with fear is to objectively face it, embrace it, allow it to pass through you and when it is over, you remain. Take some time and be honest about the fear of death in your life. As you do an honest assessment, stare into the flame of Love and allow God to speak. In the process watch the dimensions you are ascending through to hear the answer.

Gratitude
Today I am celebrating

Self - Awareness
Today I am noticing

Meditation
Did I follow through with my morning meditation ritual today   Y N

Spiritual Insight
During today's meditation I am sensed, saw, felt, learnt, experienced ...

Manifestation
Write about the day you want to have in past tense as if it has already happened.

Sketch Space

ABUNDANCE AND PROVISION VS DROUGHT

Abundance vs drought is about balancing the waters that sustain, nourish and drive life into all of creation. There are four aspects of water to consider:

1. lack of internal and external water causing drought, starvation and death
2. lack of external water which poses an opportunity for the Christian to use their inner water supply connected to heaven that never runs dry to sustain them no matter the external circumstance.
3. abundance of water causing productivity and external to flourish
4. flooding; too much water can cause death and destruction if the individual tries to control the flood.

For the purpose of this journal and meditation we are going to delve deeper into the concept of flooding.

Have you ever had a dream where you were standing on a beach or near a river and all of a sudden you look up or turn around and there is a wall of water or a tsunami headed straight for you? Did you panic? Did you run? Did you turn towards it? Did you try and stop it? In many cases (not all) how you reacted in that situation is how you would react to wealth or sudden breakthrough financially. Many people desire freedom but what if something bigger than you had the capacity to control began to come your direction?

Abundance is both exhilarating and terrifying, it undresses any veil that we would set up and exposes us at the deepest levels. Abundance, like water, can be a calm ocean that brings peace beyond what we have ever experienced or a roaring river at flood stage that cuts valleys and gorges in the hardest rock while being set against breathtaking beauty. The raw power of water, wealth and favor is something to behold. In essence it is the capacity to become the camel in the desert and to see the rain on the horizon when there are no clouds in the sky. Once upon a time I was riding in a glass top train with a good friend in the mountains outside Cusco, Peru. The train track had been built next to a river that was frequently at flood stage. The train tracks had been meticulously placed so that we were literal feet away from a rushing river and death. It was one of the best experiences of my life. The track wound with the river through the altitude of the Andes Mountains that towered over us as we beheld their beauty. Around every bend there was a new waterfall or a new snow-capped mountain that literally took our breath away. Looking at the river, it had seemingly been there since the Earth began. The smallest boulders in the river were as big as buses, the largest as big as a two- story office building. This river would laugh if someone tried to categorize it according to its rapids. It was raw, wild, untamed and almost as though God himself built it for us in that moment.

To direct the flow of finance in and out of your life requires finesse. It requires knowledge beyond what most have and many of those who master it have no idea of the depth of spiritual knowledge they are demonstrating. Directing the flow of finance in your life is directing the flow of the waters in and out of your life. The person who can govern both the internal and external waters around their life will not only accumulate abundance - they will distribute it from above.

Identity Statement

I am...

which accomplishes (associated action)

DAY	FOCUS POINT	MEDITATION PLAN
SUNDAY		
MONDAY		
TUESDAY		
WEDNESDAY		
THURSDAY		
FRIDAY		
SATURDAY		

Notes

If I was given 1 billion USD, how would I practically allocate each dollar. Giving money away is not an option. What investments would I make? What industry would I want to be involved in?

Gratitude
Today I am celebrating

Self - Awareness
Today I am noticing

Meditation   Y N
Did I follow through with my morning meditation ritual today

Spiritual Insight
During today's meditation I am sensed, saw, felt, learnt, experienced ...

Manifestation

Write about the day you want to have in past tense as if it has already happened.

Sketch Space

Everybody has a set of financial principles that they live by whether they are consciously aware of them or not. Consider your financial principles and decide whether they promote scarcity or abundance. Do they change depending on the season you are in?

Gratitude
Today I am celebrating

Self - Awareness
Today I am noticing

Meditation
Did I follow through with my morning meditation ritual today [Y] [N]

Spiritual Insight
During today's meditation I am sensed, saw, felt, learnt, experienced ...

Manifestation

Write about the day you want to have in past tense as if it has already happened.

Sketch Space

DATE & PLACE:

The most obvious application of 'abundance vs drought' is finances, however there are figurative arenas of drought and subsequent starvation vs abundance of water and fruitful lavish landscapes. Consider all the arenas in your life? Where are you producing the most, what areas feel the most lush and what areas feel like they are in drought? Can you direct more water to these areas of drought?

Gratitude
Today I am celebrating

Self - Awareness
Today I am noticing

Meditation
Y N
Did I follow through with my morning meditation ritual today

Spiritual Insight
During today's meditation I am sensed, saw, felt, learnt, experienced ...

Manifestation

Write about the day you want to have in past tense as if it has already happened.

Sketch Space

Contemplate on the Hebrew letter Gimel. Gimel is considered the camel that can maintain its own water supply even in the desert. How can you use the waters within you, connected to the waters that flow from the inner being of God, to water and maintain the abundance in all arenas of your life despite what the external circumstances are producing?

Gratitude
Today I am celebrating

Self - Awareness
Today I am noticing

Meditation
Did I follow through with my morning meditation ritual today

Y N

Spiritual Insight
During today's meditation I am sensed, saw, felt, learnt, experienced ...

Manifestation

Write about the day you want to have in past tense as if it has already happened.

Sketch Space

Uncontrollable flooding of water can seem like death and destruction to those who don't know how to operate in abundance. Consider a flash flood. For those who camp out in the dry river bed expecting it to never rain, they are swept away and die in the flash flood. In what ways do I need to become more expectant and prepare for extreme abundance and flooding? How do I create metaphorical dams and tracks for the river to flow through so that not just myself but my entire land and all the people connected to me experience abundance?

Gratitude
Today I am celebrating

Self - Awareness
Today I am noticing

Meditation   Y N
Did I follow through with my morning meditation ritual today

Spiritual Insight
During today's meditation I am sensed, saw, felt, learnt, experienced ...

Manifestation

Write about the day you want to have in past tense as if it has already happened.

Sketch Space

DATE & PLACE:

The need to control every aspect and hold all the moving parts is often the thing that causes abundance, flooding and chaos to feel like death and destruction, rather than exponential increase and blessing. What are the areas in my life where I need to surrender supreme control? What are the areas in my life that I am holding too tightly?

Gratitude
Today I am celebrating

Self - Awareness
Today I am noticing

Meditation ☐Y ☐N
Did I follow through with my morning meditation ritual today

Spiritual Insight
During today's meditation I am sensed, saw, felt, learnt, experienced ...

Manifestation

Write about the day you want to have in past tense as if it has already happened.

Sketch Space

DATE & PLACE:

Working with the angelic is critical when directing the flow of the waters both internally and externally. When you look at the waters over your life, are you aware of the angelic that are directing them? How do you interact with these angels?

Gratitude
Today I am celebrating

Self - Awareness
Today I am noticing

Meditation   Y N
Did I follow through with my morning meditation ritual today

Spiritual Insight
During today's meditation I am sensed, saw, felt, learnt, experienced ...

Manifestation

Write about the day you want to have in past tense as if it has already happened.

Sketch Space

LIGHT VS DARKNESS

There is a type of light that is connected to movement. For instance, the light of the Sun and the Moon that are connected to the cycles of the Earth. There is another type of light, light without movement that is a diffusion of light that occurs from creation's connection to God, to the blood of Jesus and the glory of the son of God. It is this light that alights the New Jerusalem (Rev) and this light that allows the very concept of life to exist within the created world. If the light of the Lamb that was slain at the foundation of the world was removed from creation, creation would wither and die.

It is from this premise that the bible commands us to obey and delight ourselves in the Word (and by proxy the Law which is an extension of the Word). By doing so we entangle ourselves with the diffused light that exists before light had movement - the light of Christ, the glory light that is emitted by the Son of God, the light of the blood that was slain and the light that sustains the New Jerusalem. "Thy word is a lamp unto thy feet and a light unto thy path," (Psalm 119:115). There is a specific light that one receives by reading the Word. A blessing that enraptures the soul, the organs, the path of man. Blessed is he whose delight is in the law of the Lord (Psalm 1), Shema Yisrael ... hearing the word and believing it causes a light of faith to enter the mind and dispel the darkness of unbelief. "And these words which I command you today shall be in your heart. You shall teach them diligently to your children, and shall talk of them when you sit in your house, when you walk by the way, when you lie down, and when you rise up You shall bind them as a sign on your hand, and they shall be as frontlets between your eyes. You shall write them on the doorposts of your house and on your gates." (Deuteronomy 6)

In contrast, darkness is an interesting concept in the Bible and takes on various forms. There is darkness that is a closing off of the light of God to something. The soul that is not illuminated by the Word. The closing off of light is a serious thing. When the light of God gets closed off, there is no access to joy or to the presence. This darkness reveals evil and causes a shadow to fall upon whatever the light is closed off towards. However, there is also darkness that is the invisibility of something as it is hidden and of course the mysteries of God that are concealed rather than revealed.

One of the many things we are exploring in this endeavor is the mysteries of God that are concealed. "It is the glory of The Lord to conceal a matter and the glory of Kings to search it out". The invisibility of something in anyone's life is either a "not yet" because you are not mature enough or, more than likely, an invitation to explore and mature along the way. Darkness can be a beautiful thing as it can reveal the secrets. Now, if only we knew how to keep from projecting every little thing God shows us to the world and learned to keep silent, it is probable that God would share more with us. The balancing of light and dark within one's life personally might be a balancing of that which is concealed and that which is revealed. A mature person becomes the vault that can be entrusted with the deeper things of God, only revealing them to trusted students with permission from above.

Identity Statement

I am...

....

....

which accomplishes (associated action)

....

....

DAY	FOCUS POINT	MEDITATION PLAN
SUNDAY		
MONDAY		
TUESDAY		
WEDNESDAY		
THURSDAY		
FRIDAY		
SATURDAY		

Notes

....

....

....

DATE & PLACE:

How does Jesus, who is the Word, infuse light into all of my being,? How does reading the Word, engaging the Hebrew letters (letters of light) continue to infuse that light into me?

Gratitude
Today I am celebrating

Self - Awareness
Today I am noticing

Meditation

Y N

Did I follow through with my morning meditation ritual today

Spiritual Insight
During today's meditation I am sensed, saw, felt, learnt, experienced ...

Manifestation
Write about the day you want to have in past tense as if it has already happened.

Sketch Space

There are multiple Bible verses about writing the law (which is an extension of the word) onto your heart, binding to your hand and head. Why does the Bible attach light to these specific points? What is the value of light saturating the head, heart and hand for man?

Gratitude
Today I am celebrating

Self - Awareness
Today I am noticing

Meditation
Did I follow through with my morning meditation ritual today

Y N

Spiritual Insight
During today's meditation I am sensed, saw, felt, learnt, experienced ...

Manifestation

Write about the day you want to have in past tense as if it has already happened.

Sketch Space

There is an ability of light and being wrapped by the light of Christ that allows one to be concealed? What is the value of concealment for me personally? What is the value of limiting my exposure and not exhibiting all of what I contain to everyone?

Gratitude
Today I am celebrating

Self - Awareness
Today I am noticing

Meditation
Did I follow through with my morning meditation ritual today   Y N

Spiritual Insight
During today's meditation I am sensed, saw, felt, learnt, experienced ...

Manifestation

Write about the day you want to have in past tense as if it has already happened.

Sketch Space

There is a concept of light before movement, the light that exists prior to creation and the cycles of the Sun and Moon. It is like a radiating light similar to the light that occurs as the result of the Lamb of God in the New Jerusalem. How do I engage this form of light and allow it to diffuse into all of my being? What would it mean to be cut off from this light? Is that even possible?

Gratitude
Today I am celebrating

Self - Awareness
Today I am noticing

Meditation
Y N

Did I follow through with my morning meditation ritual today

Spiritual Insight
During today's meditation I am sensed, saw, felt, learnt, experienced ...

Manifestation
Write about the day you want to have in past tense as if it has already happened.

Sketch Space

There is a specific type of light that is connected with glory that is diffused into all of creation. What would creation have looked like if the light of glory had not been congealed during the fall of man? What would the rocks look like? The animals? The plants? The inorganic and organic?

Gratitude
Today I am celebrating

Self - Awareness
Today I am noticing

Meditation
Did I follow through with my morning meditation ritual today

Spiritual Insight
During today's meditation I am sensed, saw, felt, learnt, experienced ...

Manifestation
Write about the day you want to have in past tense as if it has already happened.

Sketch Space

What does it mean to be considered the entrusted one? There is a principle of being entrusted by God with the mysteries that is embedded into the construct of concealed and revealed. How does this integrate with my ego and my understanding of the responsibility I carry for handling the deeper things?

Gratitude
Today I am celebrating

Self - Awareness
Today I am noticing

Meditation   Y N
Did I follow through with my morning meditation ritual today

Spiritual Insight
During today's meditation I am sensed, saw, felt, learnt, experienced ...

Manifestation
Write about the day you want to have in past tense as if it has already happened.

Sketch Space

As we move between the light and mystery, there is a concept of concealment and being revealed. If what we are revealing or what aspect of ourselves is to be revealed could be done perfectly, what would it look like? What are the steps needed in order to steward what we have learned well? How does the revealing of ourselves effect the people around us and how do we love them well through our revealing, especially when the part of us they relate is passing away and our own newness is coming?

Gratitude
Today I am celebrating

Self - Awareness
Today I am noticing

Meditation   Y N
Did I follow through with my morning meditation ritual today

Spiritual Insight
During today's meditation I am sensed, saw, felt, learnt, experienced ...

Manifestation
Write about the day you want to have in past tense as if it has already happened.

Sketch Space

Joseph C Sturgeon II

The established revealing of light and enlightenment in your life is a dimensional reality very few have been able to express (outside art and anime). Even then, on a personal level it is difficult to describe other than waking up to the best day of your life every moment you take a breath to focus on something different. The beauty, the honor, the life, the love, the fulfillment, the joy, the strength and everything in between come, even for a moment, in perpetuity. John the Revelator said it best in Revelation 4:11; "You are worthy, our Lord and our God to receive Glory, Honor and Power. For you created all things and by your will they existed and were created."

ADDITIONAL PROMPTS

Week 1: Judgement and Mercy
- How does a King judge?
- How does a King show mercy?
- Is there a situation where both are shown and apply?
- What has judgement looked like in your life?
- Where have I seen the principle of the universal balancing of scales in other religions, sectors of life, zodiac?
- What do the words 'fair' and 'equal' mean to me and how much value do I place on these components? Do I feel deeply offended when I consider something "unfair"? How do these concepts interact with my perception of grace?
- I thought Jesus took all of that? What parts did he take and what parts did he not take upon himself?
- What is the difference between judgement that comes from The Father and judgement that comes from the world and our actions?
- When does mercy become too much? Cause harm?
- At what point does mercy leave that which I am called to protect vulnerable?
- With what aspects of compassion does God see the world through?
- Focus on one aspect of compassion and begin to integrate it into your
- engagements. How does it change the engagement?

Week 2: Life, Death, Sacrifice, Surrender, Health and Resurrection
- What does it mean to die daily?
- How does the blood of Jesus Christ cause multiplication and in what dimensions does that multiplication occur?
- When did Adam learn the principle of resurrection, if there was no death or decay in heaven? Did he learn it after the fall?
- What is the connection between sleep and death? Did sleep in Heaven look like it does now on Earth? Consider Isaiah's words "Awake o sleeper and rise from the dead"? (Isaiah 60:1; Ephesian 5:14)
- How can I balance my spiritual health with my natural health?
- How does my natural health effect my spiritual health?
- How does my physical breath and level of stress impact my ability to move in the spirit?

Week 3: Abundance and drought

- What does abundance look like for you?
- How can I turn what I currently have into abundance?
- What emotional trigger do I have that causes me to spend money like crazy? Out of the following list of advertising strategies of persuasion (reciprocity - feeling like I need to give after I have received; social proof - using the mass majority for validation; authority- trustworthy and credible; scarcity - last one left; exclusivity - one of a kind and consistency - sticking with previous choices) which marketing tool am I most susceptible to and in which arena in my life?
- What percentage of my profits and gains do I get to spend on myself? What is my own reward structure?
- How can I protect myself against an unsure market or economic downturn?
- How can I better prepare for the next drought?
- Is drought necessary? Why or why not?
- Do I need to be managing my own finances? Why or why not?
- Who can I employ that can help me with my future?
- How do I increase the flow of water into my life? How can I increase the rate of connection between the waters in my life and the waters that proceed from the throne of God? Does all water have to move through my heart or can it bypass it and flow directly towards my hand?
- After the figurative flood, what are the signs that there is dry land ahead?

Week 4: Light, enlightenment, darkness and mystery

- What was the darkness that God created in Genesis 1?
- What does spiritual light do?
- What is the difference between light and enlightenment?
- What is the difference between darkness and mystery?
- What else does the darkness that God created contain other than mystery?
- What happens when the Light shines on you?
- What are the different areas of enlightenment?
- Why are there polarities like light and darkness, enlightenment and mystery?
- Do these polarities exist in the upper realms of Heaven? Why or why not?
- Where does the light sit within you and what is the process through which light reveals enlightenment?

ABOUT THE AUTHOR

Joseph Sturgeon lives and works in Alabama. He loves spending time in heaven and recording these experiences in writing.

Otherwise you will find him enjoying the outdoors, being involved in the business world and traveling with friends.

More resources can be found at www.revelationrevealed.net

Heaven's Heart for Earth

Seraph Creative is a collective of artists, writers, theologians & illustrators who desire to see the body of Christ grow into full maturity, walking in their inheritance as Sons Of God on the Earth.

Sign up to our newsletter to know about the release of the next book in the series as well as other exciting releases.

Visit our website :

www.seraphcreative.org